getting into

Oxford
&
Cambridge

trotman

getting into

Oxford
&
Cambridge

Natalie Lancer

11th edition

Getting into Oxford & Cambridge

This 11th edition published in 2008 by Trotman Publishing, an imprint of Crimson Publishing Limited, Westminster House, Kew Road, Richmond, Surrey TW9 2ND.

© Trotman 1987, 1989, 1991, 1994, 1996, 1999, 2001, 2003, 2005, 2007. Reprinted 2005, 2006, 2007, 2008.

Author Natalie Lancer

Previous editions written by Sarah Alakija

British Library Cataloguing in Publication Data
A catalogue record for this book is available from the British Library

ISBN 978 1 84455 165 1

Typeset by Newgen Imaging Systems Pvt Ltd.

Printed and bound by The Cromwell Press, Trowbridge, Wiltshire.

Contents

About the author

Natalie Lancer went to the University of Oxford and graduated in Oriental Studies: Hebrew and Arabic. She was the Director of Studies at MPW and currently is the Assistant Principal at a school in West London.

Introduction

In order to get the most out this book you need to interact with it. This involves following up relevant web pages, reading them for yourselves, filling in the tables and going on the visits as suggested. It is important to remember that every applicant has or will have three or four As at A level or equivalent qualifications, every applicant has loads of interesting personal qualities and that there are a limited number of places. Therefore, even if you are an outstanding candidate, there are many outstanding candidates and your place is not guaranteed. However, by following the advice in this book you will give yourself the best possible chance.

It is sad, but true, that even if you put yourself in the best possible position to get a place, you may still be unsuccessful. But, take heart, there are many excellent universities and if you really are outstanding you will have an interesting and fulfilling life whatever you do. However, let's get going on with maximising your chances of entry into Oxford and Cambridge. As with many things, it is best to plan ahead. Ideally you should be reading this in your first year of Sixth Form. This is because unlike applications to other universities, which can continue up until January in your A2 year without penalty (you can apply after January but the universities are not under any obligation to give your application the same consideration) the deadline for application for Oxford and Cambridge is 15 October of your A2 year – extremely early in the first term. In other words, the bulk of the preparation has to be done in the previous term and throughout the summer.

The aim of this book is not to reproduce information that is readily available and indeed you should read on the Oxford and Cambridge admissions websites, but to explain how to access and how to use this information and, most importantly, how to make sense of it. By working though the exercises in this book, you will put yourself in the best possible position to get a place at Oxford or Cambridge.

The first thing you should do is to order the undergraduate prospectus for both universities. Although all the available information is online as well, and I will make frequent reference to these websites, it is often easier to see the information in paper form. To order the prospectuses, ring the Oxford Colleges Admissions Office on 01865 288000, or email undergraduate.admissions@admin.ox.ac.uk or order online at www.ox.ac.uk/admissions/prospectuses.html.

Ring the Cambridge Admissions Office on 01223 333308, email at admissions@cam.ac.uk or order online at www.cam.ac.uk/admissions/undergraduate/publications/prospectus.html.

In addition, the Student Unions at both universities write an 'alternative prospectus' and these will give you another perspective of life at the university. See www.ousu.org/prospective-students/ap and www.cusu.cam.ac.uk/prospective/prospectus.

Checklist

Have you understood?

☐ You are going to have to interact with this book.

Follow it up

☐ Have you ordered both the Oxford and Cambridge prospectuses?

01 Choosing a university, choosing a college

■ Should I apply to Oxbridge?

It is often said that Oxbridge is a 'self-selection' process. This means that the people who consider going are the people who should be considering it. Your teacher may have suggested it to you, maybe you know someone who went or maybe you have read about it or seen a film where they feature. Whatever the situation, you have realised that there is something special about *Oxbridge* (the word used to describe Oxford and Cambridge collectively) and you are wondering if it is for you. The short answer is: it probably is. Why? Because there are so many different types of colleges that make up Oxford and Cambridge, from traditional to avant garde, historic to modern, left wing to right wing, that there is bound to be one that suits you. It is important to realise that students at Oxford or Cambridge work extremely hard. Typically you will write at least one essay of about 2,500 words a week for a tutorial (Oxford) or a supervision (Cambridge). Although it will vary between subjects, in your first year you will have lectures to attend (for sciences about three hours a day and for arts maybe five hours a week) and perhaps a small technical class to attend. For some subjects lectures are optional. In the second and third years you have more choice over what to attend. You will be given book and journal lists and a lot of time will be spent undertaking independent study. There are also exams (called Collections at Oxford) at the beginning of every term in Oxford and at the end of each year at Cambridge.

Oxford and Cambridge welcome students from all ethnic and financial backgrounds, with disabilities, with children and also mature students. The next section is concerned with the practicalities of this.

■ Can I afford to go to Oxbridge?

Most universities, including Oxford and Cambridge, charge £3,145 (correct for 2009 entry) for annual tuition fees which will increase in line with inflation. You can get a student loan to cover the cost of the fees which you do not have to repay until after you have graduated and are earning a salary of £15,000 or more. There are also living costs that cannot be deferred. This includes rent, clothes and food. Both universities provide college accommodation (although the length of time they provide it varies considerably between colleges), which is substantially cheaper than commercial rates, and you only have to pay it when you are 'in residence' and not in your holidays. A typical rent is between £65 and £80 per week for a room for 30 weeks and for an ensuite room between £80 and £100 per week. Meals in college are heavily subsidised and are usually of excellent quality. In fact, Merton College in Oxford was endowed with a sum of money by one of its alumni to ensure the food was of top quality. It is important to understand that you can go to Oxford or Cambridge regardless of your family's financial circumstances.

Straight from the horse's mouth

Both Oxford and Cambridge are very keen to make it clear that if you need financial assistance, they will give it to you. The back of the Oxford Prospectus says:

If you can get in, we can help out . . . At Oxford your mind is the only asset we're interested in. Oxford Opportunity Bursaries are worth up to £13k over four years and available to anyone whose family income is below £38k.

Oxford Prospectus, 2008

The Cambridge Prospectus describes the Cambridge Bursary Scheme:

We are committed to the principle that no UK student should be deterred from applying to the University of Cambridge because of financial concerns, and that no student should have to leave because of financial difficulties. As a result we have one of the most extensive financial support programmes in the UK to ensure that students can meet the cost of the Cambridge education, regardless of background.

Cambridge Prospectus, 2008

In addition, most of the colleges themselves are very rich and provide their own bursaries, grants and scholarships. They also give prizes (which mean financial rewards) for academic excellence in tutorials/ supervisions and exams. Telephone the colleges individually to find out what is on offer.

If you are lucky enough to be a near professional singer or organist and would like to spend at least six hours a week singing in the college chapel or playing the organ, you can also apply for a music or choral award. The application deadline for this is a month earlier than for regular undergraduate UCAS applications. See 'Key dates' (Appendix 2). See www.admissions.ox.ac.uk/orgscholars and http://131.111.8.46/admissions/undergraduate/musicawards/index.html for more information.

Some colleges interview music or choral scholars in September and others in December. There are also different requirements for music or choral scholars at different colleges. For example, you may have to be trained in the Anglican tradition or may have to be the right kind of baritone.

Mature students

A mature student is defined as someone who is 21 by 1 October of the year in which they start their course. If you are a mature student, you may prefer one of the colleges that admits a good number of mature students or exclusively admits mature students (see tables at back of book).

Young students

There is no minimum age for applicants, but the university will want you to demonstrate that you have the maturity to study in a university environment. If you will be younger than 18 in the year of entry it may be best to take a year out and improve your life skills.

Students who want to take a gap year

If you want to take a gap year and you have something concrete and worthwhile that you want to do in it, then taking a gap year will not be an issue. If you are applying for languages and you haven't studied one of the languages before, the admissions tutors might even encourage you to take a gap year. Conversely, if you are applying for Maths, the admissions tutor may feel that you may forget your Maths and may need some reassuring that what you are doing in your gap year will augment your studies and not help you forget them. Policies about gap years vary between individual colleges and subjects and so if you know you want to have a gap year, consult the admissions tutor well in advance. That said, if they think you are good, they won't mind if you take a gap year, if you can demonstrate how it will be useful and productive.

Straight from the horse's mouth

About one in five students coming to Cambridge takes a gap year before starting their studies. This year out proves a very useful time in which to improve skills, earn money, travel and generally gain maturity and self-reliance.

Cambridge Prospectus, 2007/8

■ Disabled students

Disabled students are welcomed at both universities. There may be some practical considerations such as making sure you choose a college that is near to your faculty so that you will not have to walk far. The admissions offices at both universities can help you with this so be sure to telephone them as early as possible. Of course, there are a whole range of disabilities which include dyslexia and visual or hearing impairments. The disability must be declared on the UCAS form. In no way are people who declare a disability at a disadvantage. The key is to contact the admissions office as early as possible.

Straight from the horse's mouth

We have an excellent Disability Resource Centre at Cambridge, and we would encourage any student who may need support if they gain admission here to contact the DRC well before they are interviewed.

Admissions Tutor, Cambridge

■ Student parents

Both Oxford and Cambridge welcome applications from prospective students who have children. There are several colleges that provide accommodation for couples and families. You should ring up the admissions office to find this out. Also, some colleges have their own nurseries (see tables at back of book). There are also some university-wide nurseries.

■ Students from ethnic minorities

Cambridge is taking active steps to particularly welcome students from ethnic minorities. The group to encourage ethnic minority applications (GEEMA) has been set up. Email geema@cao.cam.ac.uk and the Oxford Admissions office for more information.

■ International students

International students are welcomed at both Oxford and Cambridge. International students make up less than 10% of undergraduates at Cambridge and 14% of undergraduates at Oxford. However, the percentages of overseas students are much higher for postgraduate study: at Cambridge 50% of postgraduates and at Oxford 63% of postgraduates are international students. In order to study at Oxford and Cambridge, your English must be of a high standard. This is measured by your performance in the IELTS (International English

Language Testing System) exam: you need a score of at least 7.0 in each section (speaking, listening, writing and reading) or a GCSE in English Language at grade C or above. See the university prospectus for more details. The costs of studying at a UK university for an international student are much higher than for a 'home' student. The tuition fees range from £9,327 to £12,219 for most courses although Clinical Medicine costs in excess of £20,000. See http://131.111.8.46/admissions/undergraduate/international/costs.htm and www.admissions.ox.ac.uk/finance/costs/#uni for more details about costs and www.ilets.org for more information about the IELTS exam and where it can be sat.

Gay, lesbian, bisexual, transsexual (GLBT) students

Oxford and Cambridge are totally pluralist universities. Not only is there a central GLBT society but each college also has its own GLBT society. There are plenty of events to make you feel totally comfortable.

Straight from the horse's mouth

Perhaps it is worth reminding yourself that:

We can't offer you a place if you don't apply.

Cambridge Prospectus, 2007/8

Oxford or Cambridge?

First off, let's be clear, you can apply to Oxford *or* Cambridge but not both. They are both as prestigious as each other and both have wonderful facilities such as a plethora of world-class libraries and world-class teaching. So how do you decide which one to apply to?

Choosing a university by subject offered

There are various subjects that Oxford offers that Cambridge does not and vice versa.

Subjects you can study at Cambridge but not at Oxford:

- Architecture
- Economics (as a stand-alone subject in Oxford you do a combined course of Economics and Management)
- Education Studies
- Land Economy
- Languages: Dutch, Anglo-Saxon, Norse and Celtic

- Management Studies (as a stand-alone subject in Oxford you do a combined course of Economics and Management)
- Natural Sciences (although at Oxford all the sciences are offered but not in the same combination)
- Philosophy (as a stand-alone subject in Oxford you do a combined course of PPE)
- SPS (Social and Political Science)
- Veterinary Medicine.

Subjects you can study at Oxford but not at Cambridge:

- Languages: Sanskrit, Czech with Slovak
- PPE (Philosophy, Politics and Economics)
- PPP (Psychology, Philosophy and Physiology)
- Separate sciences although you do have to do modules in other science subjects as well.

Subjects you can study at both universities:

- All the sciences
- Archaeology and Anthropology
- Classics
- Computer Science
- Engineering
- English
- Geography
- History
- Human Sciences
- Law
- Modern and Medieval Languages
- Music
- Oriental Studies (at Oxford) and Asian and Middle Eastern Studies Course (at Cambridge)
- Theology and Religious Studies.

To see which courses are offered at Oxford and Cambridge go to: www.admissions.ox.ac.uk and www.cam.ac.uk/admissions/undergraduate respectively.

If both universities offer the same course, how can you decide which one to apply for? First, it is very important to understand that just because the title is the same, it does not mean the course is the same. For example, Economics can be studied at both Oxford and Cambridge, but at Oxford it is either within the PPE or Economics and Management course. The Economics modules in Economics and Management are influenced by Management, so if you take a Finance module it would be mathematically based but within Management. There is great flexibility as to which modules you can take. At Cambridge, Economics is the main course. The founder of Macroeconomics (Keynes) went to Cambridge and the course is more traditional. Economics at Cambridge has more compulsory mathematical elements than that at Oxford although one can opt to do mathematical options at Oxford.

It is important to read the course details carefully, which can be found in the prospectus or in the online prospectus, so that you can make an informed decision as to which course would be more suitable for you.

The next step is to go on an open day or to walk round the universities and colleges, which will be discussed below.

■ Open days

Both universities run open days throughout the year but mainly between April and July of your AS year. You can find out when they are at www.admissions.ox.ac.uk/opendays/open1.html and www.cam.ac.uk/admissions/undergraduate/opendays. The next step is to ring up the college or faculty and book yourself a place. Although the faculties also conduct open days, it will be much more informative to sign up for a college open day. It does not matter which college you choose and you will get to visit your chosen faculty as well as seeing the college.

Each of the two universities is made up of many colleges. The course content of the subject is set centrally at the university level. The university is the equivalent of the Exam boards and they also provide lectures in large lecture halls for you to attend and practicals where applicable. Sometimes these are optional and sometimes these are compulsory – it depends on the subject.

The colleges are a bit like boarding school. You live and eat there and you also get taught by your tutors there in tutorials/supervisions or in classes. If your college does not have a specialist in a particular part of the course then you may go to another college for that part or in a small faculty you will be taught in that faculty. The faculties and colleges occupy different sites at the universities and you will have to walk or cycle between them.

What are you meant to be looking for at an open day?

First you are going to get an overall impression of the place. Walk to the library and to your faculty buildings (use the map at the back of this book). How far away are they from your proposed college? Would you prefer to be at a college that is on the river or that is near the library? Do you want to be at a sporty college? Ask any students that you find how they like their college.

The open day is also an opportunity to meet the tutors and ask them some questions. You can really make an impression on them at this point so make sure you are smartly dressed and you ask sensible questions. You may want to know about aspects of the course. You could ask them to recommend a book for you to read. Try to find a student who is on your course and ask them what it is like.

You will normally get a talk from the dean (like a headmaster) of the college and a tour of the faculty. You will almost certainly be given lunch for free. Your school may also organise trips to Oxford or Cambridge for which you should sign up. If you miss the open days and your school does not do trips to both universities then just go up for the day and look around yourself. The maps at the back of this book should help you.

When you visit the colleges, make sure you tell the college porters that you are a prospective student and that your parent/friend is accompanying you as otherwise you may be asked to pay a tourist entrance fee which you do not need to pay. Be insistent on this point even if the porter still wants to charge you – ask to see the head porter if necessary. Tourists pay at least £3 per person per college which can work out to be rather expensive considering there are about 40 colleges. Some colleges are for graduates only so it is necessary to do some research and plan your route before you go. Many colleges are clustered together but some are further away.

Ultimately, you have to be able to see yourself at your chosen college. After the formal proceedings of the open day have concluded visit other colleges and write down your impressions using the table at the back of this book. Once you have a short list you can fill in other aspects of the college using the prospectus such as how many years it offers accommodation for in college.

Over to you

- When you walk round the colleges fill in the table at the back of this book.
- Ask a student the following question: if they weren't at their college, which college would they have chosen?

However, ultimately your college choice is not too important. Many candidates get 'pooled' at interview and may not end up at their chosen college (see Chapter 8). Everyone likes their college in the end!

■ Choosing a college

Criteria for choosing a college

Oxford has 30 colleges and six permanent private halls and Cambridge has 29 colleges – so how do you choose a college to which to apply? Students admitted to permanent private halls are full members of the university and for all intents and purposes they are the same as colleges. They are often very old and have a different sort of history to the colleges. Subjects offered tend to be Philosophy and Theology and at some of the permanent private halls many of the students are planning to be ordained as priests. Some do have entry restrictions but most will accept applications from people of any cultural background. I have included some brief notes about them for completeness in the table shown in Appendix 4 (See page 104).

You should read through the description of each college. Not all colleges offer all subjects and you should find out what subjects are not offered in the general prospectus. Oxford produces a handy table that summarises this information at www.admissions.ox.ac.uk/colleges/availab. pdf. For Cambridge you will have to click on each college separately (this may be easier by reading the hard copy of the prospectus that you have ordered).

In addition there are two more prospectuses you can consult. When you have narrowed your choices down a little, contact each college individually and ask for a copy of their college prospectus. This will give you more of a flavour of the college. It will tell you what clubs, societies, sports facilities and traditions they have (although remember that most clubs and societies are run centrally and there are hundreds to sign up to!). Each JCR (Junior Common Room) also produces a student written 'alternative prospectus' which is less formal and gives you an idea of the student perspective of the college. Again contact the college or ask for the email of the JCR president to order a copy. All prospectuses will be sent to you free of charge.

There are various factors that you may like to consider when choosing a college. Would you prefer to spend three or four years in a small college where you will get to know everyone in all years (about 40 people in each year) or would you prefer to be in a large college (about 120 people in each year). Would you like to live near the city centre (remember that both Oxford and Cambridge are both very small anyway) or further away? Colleges that are further away tend to have a very close-knit atmosphere as people socialise in college a lot more. If you like sleeping in, would you like your college to be near your faculty so you can roll out of bed to attend lectures?

You might like to find out the gender balance. When you visit the college, ask a student what is the male–female ratio. It used to be until relatively recently that all colleges were single sex. Some colleges still have a legacy of this in that some former male colleges have a greater ratio of men to women. You can also look up this statistic in the prospectus or online. Some colleges are known to have a political bent, for example, King's (Cambridge) and Wadham (Oxford) are generally considered to be left wing whereas Peterhouse (Cambridge) and Christ Church (Oxford) are considered to be more traditional. Does the library have long opening hours (some libraries open 24 hours a day). What is the undergraduate–graduate ratio? Has the food in hall (the dining room) got a good or bad reputation?

You might look at what the ratio is between state school–non-state school, although this may be unimportant. All colleges are now committed to encouraging students from all types of schools to attend. Looking at the published tables is very interesting in this regard.

Do you want to be in a college with old or modern buildings? It is important to find out if the college offers accommodation for the duration of your studies or whether you will have to go to find a house to share after the first year. Some people like living in a house with their friends but there are associated problems: landlords that do not sort out broken central heating quickly, houses that are far away from your college. Also remember that often, colleges can accommodate you in student flats which you can share with your friends and the college will look after you much better than a land-lord. Most college accommodation is in single rooms, perhaps with an ensuite bathroom, but more usually shared bathrooms on one staircase (perhaps 10 individual rooms on a staircase).

You may like to take a less emotional approach to choosing a college and look at the league tables that rank colleges according to how well the undergraduates did in their final exams, that are published by various newspapers including *The Sunday Times University Guide*. (In Cambridge it is called the Tompkins Table and in Oxford it is called the Norrington Table.) Degrees obtained at the college are scored in the following way: five points for a first; three for a 2:1; two for a 2:2 and one for a third. The score shown is the percentage of total points available.

Norrington Table 2007.[a]

College rank 2007	College	Norrington score 2007 (%)
1	Merton	76.63
2	Magdalen	74.81
3	Christ Church	73.23
4	Balliol	73.10
5	New College	72.46
6	St John's	71.64
7	Trinity	71.36
8	Lincoln	70.57
9	Hertford	70.20
10	Pembroke	69.47
11	Worcester	69.08
12	St Edmund Hall	68.67

13	St Anne's	68.50
14	University	68.38
15	Jesus	68.28
16	Queen's	67.76
17	Wadham	67.37
18	Keble	66.92
19	Somerville	66.27
20	St Peter's	66.10
21	Brasenose	65.98
22	Lady Margaret Hall	65.94
23	Corpus Christi	65.48
24	Exeter	65.27
25	St Hugh's	65.25
26	St Catherine's	65.15
27	St Hilda's	64.88
28	Mansfield	64.13
29	Oriel	63.46
30	Harris Manchester	53.64

[a] College undergraduate degree classifications 2007 (sorted by rank).

Source: University of Oxford.

Tompkins Table 2007.

College rank 2007	College	Tompkins score (%)
1	Emmanuel	66.62
2	Christ's	66.33
3	Downing	66.18
4	Selwyn	66.12
5	St Catharine's	66.10
6	Trinity	65.87
7	Pembroke	65.60
8	Corpus Christi	65.57
9	Jesus	65.47
10	Gonville & Caius	65.03
11	Queens'	64.25
12	Sidney Sussex	64.11
13	Magdalene	63.98
14	Fitzwilliam	63.96
15	Churchill	63.76
16	Trinity Hall	63.36
17	Clare	62.63

(Continued)

Tompkins Table 2007 (Continued).

College rank 2007	College	Tompkins score (%)
18	King's	62.37
19	St John's	61.82
20	Robinson	61.25
21	Girton	61.06
22	Newnham	59.99
23	New Hall	59.37
24	Lucy Cavendish	58.92
25	Peterhouse	58.85
26	Homerton	58.33
27	Wolfson	55.92
28	St Edmund's	51.57
29	Hughes Hall	49.38

Source: Peter Tompkins.

Permanent Private Hall Undergraduate Degree Classifications 2006/7 (sorted alphabetically).

PPH	Norrington score 2007 (%)	PPH rank 2007
Regent's Park College	60.00	3
Campion Hall	51.43	5
St Benet's Hall	65.33	1
St Stephen's House	40.00	6
Wycliffe Hall	63.75	2

A statistic that is not very helpful provided in the prospectuses is how many people applied per place per subject per college. The undiscerning person may think the way to guarantee your place at Oxford or Cambridge is to apply to the place that had the lowest ratio of applicants to places. However, if everyone thought that, then the place that had the lowest ratio of applicants to places that year would then have the highest. The more interesting question is which subjects are the most competitive. The important thing to remember is this – if you are good, you might not get into your first choice college but you also may be pooled. You are going to spend three or four years in this college and it is important that you really like the college and are not going there for the wrong reasons. If you are insistent on looking at this information go to www.admin.cam.ac.uk/univ/camdata; www.cam.ac.uk/admissions/undergraduate/statistics; www.cam.ac.uk/admissions/undergraduate/statistics/index.html.

Open applications

If after all your research, you still don't feel a particular pull to one more than another, you can make an 'open' application. An 'open application' is one where you do not specify a college and the admissions computer will assign you to a college that is undersubscribed in your subject. If there is a college that you really do not want to go to, do not put in an 'open application' as you may get sent there and there is nothing you can do about it. 15% of students in Oxford make 'open applications' and the success rates are the same for college-specific applications.

Straight from the horse's mouth

If an applicant makes an open application and the statistical programme allocates that candidate to our college, the candidate will be treated as if they applied directly to our college.

Admissions Tutor, Cambridge

Do not spend an excessive amount of time agonising over choosing a college otherwise your work may begin to suffer and if you don't get those As you won't be going to any college.

Straight from the horse's mouth

It is worth bearing in mind that:

Cooperative arrangements between the colleges are designed to ensure that able candidates applying to oversubscribed college are placed at other colleges. Almost 20% of successful candidates are placed at a college other than their college of preference each year.

Oxford Prospectus, 2008

Choosing a course

Some people just seem to know what they want to study. If you are not sure then get some advice from your careers advisor or teacher. I suggest to my students going to the admissions page of a big university such as Manchester and going through the courses from A–Z (www.manchester.ac.uk), clicking on the ones of which you have not heard and those of which you have heard and want to find out more. Make a short list of about ten and construct a table. Next to each subject write down the A-level subject entry requirements. Find out as much about the course as possible. Look up these subjects at Oxford and Cambridge if they do them and compare the course structure. How is it different? Which parts are emphasised? There are some courses that can be done at other universities that are not on offer at Oxford or Cambridge so you may have to think about what you want to do.

■ Changing subjects

At Oxford, you apply for your subject and normally students continue to study that subject for the duration of their time at university. That is not to say that the focus is narrow, there are many options within your subject you can choose and options increase as you go from year to year. Also it is not unheard of to change subjects after your first year provided you can have a good reason, have passed your first year exams and can demonstrate a deep interest and commitment to your new subject. Changing subjects is at the discretion of your college.

At Cambridge there is a more formalised approach to changing subjects and perhaps a wider recognition that students may change their mind about what they want to study or a recognition that students may want to study more than one subject that may or may not be related to each other. This approach is called the Tripos system. Subjects are split into Part 1 (which takes one or sometimes two years depending on the subject), Part 2 (which also takes one or two years depending on the subject) and in some cases also Part 3. All courses last at least three years, sometimes four and if subjects include Clinical Studies such as Medicine or Veterinary Science, even six years. Most students go to Cambridge and think they want to study one subject. If after a year, they want to change their subject, for example, to Law, they have to notify their college and then they join a two-year law course specially designed for people who have changed subject. The three-year law degree has been crammed into two years so it is hard work, but you graduate in Law just as someone who studies Law from the beginning of their degree would graduate. In fact, you can only take certain subjects such as Linguistics, Chemical Engineering, Manufacturing Engineering and History and Philosophy of Science as a Part II and you cannot apply for it for your first-year course. A small number of students may apply to Cambridge and already know that they want to do one year of one subject and then change to another subject. If they are confident that they can show commitment to both subjects and can justify why they want to do it, they should write their intentions on the Supplementary Application Questionnaire. You may come out of Cambridge with two Part Is in two subjects, a Part I and a Part II in two related subjects or a Part I and a Part II in unrelated subjects. It very much depends on the subjects you choose. You will not be disadvantaged knowing you what you want to do in Part II and if you change your mind later on – that is fine.

■ Checklist

Have you understood?

☐ Oxford and Cambridge cost the same as most universities in the UK?

Follow it up

Have you . . .

- [ ] Booked yourself onto an open day?
- [ ] Researched which colleges offer your subject?
- [ ] Filled in the table at the back of the book comparing the colleges?

02 Entry requirements

▪ Qualifications

In order to apply to Oxford or Cambridge you will need excellent marks in A level or International Baccalaureate, Scottish Highers or any other qualification that Oxford or Cambridge accepts.

You will also need excellent grades in your GCSEs or your country's equivalent qualification. Typically you need about 5–6 A's at GCSE. The subjects are less important in the case of GCSE than A levels and you have probably already taken your GCSEs at this point. If you haven't, then in addition to English (Language and/or Literature), Maths and Science, I can recommend doing the following:

- At least one language
- At least one humanities subject (Geography, History or Religious Studies)
- You don't need to but you could do a practical subject, for example, Art, ICT (Information and Communication Technology), Design Technology (clearly if you want to apply to Oxford to read Fine Art you will need to do Art and if you want to do Computation you may opt to do ICT).

If you follow this you will have a broad foundation for your A levels or further qualifications, enabling you to take any subject at A level. If you do not take a range of GCSEs you will be limiting your choices at A level. It is also important to show that at this foundation level, you are an all-rounder. This is not a necessary thing to show at A level but remember that GCSEs are quite basic.

I don't have five or six A*s at GCSE

There may be several reasons for this. Maybe you are a late academic bloomer or maybe you have only just started taking your studies seriously. If you fall into either of these categories, as long as you go the extra mile or hundred miles at the A-level stage you may still be in with a chance (see later). However, if you are reading this book in your GCSE year, or before, the best thing you can do is to work really hard with a good study regime and do really well in your GCSEs.

A levels

Straight from the horse's mouth

'Nobody predicted less than three As at A level has a chance, A*s at GCSE matter a lot.'

Admissions Tutor, Oxford

If you are lucky enough to go to a very supportive school, you will probably get a lot of guidance about your A-level choices, particularly in light of the fact that you are thinking of applying to Oxford or Cambridge. If you are not so lucky, then don't worry, this book will help you make the right decision.

First of all, you need to acknowledge that there is a 'currency' in A levels. An A level in Media Studies is not (rightly or wrongly) worth the same as an A level in Chemistry. I remember sitting in the room when a Science teacher was trying to sell Applied Science Double A level as an alternative to taking Chemistry and Biology for a prospective medical student but the truth is Applied Science Double A level does not have the same gravitas as Chemistry or Biology A level, even if your Head of Science thinks it does.

Acceptable A levels

- Art
- Biology
- Chemistry
- Classical Civilisation
- Design and Technology
- English Language and Literature
- English Literature
- Further Maths
- Geography
- Government and Politics
- Greek
- History
- History of Art
- Latin
- Mathematics
- Modern Languages
- Music
- Physics
- Politics
- Religious Studies
- Sociology

This list is not exhaustive. If you are unsure or your A level has not appeared on this list, telephone/email the admissions office for the university (numbers supplied at the end of the introduction of this book).

'Unacceptable' or 'soft-option' A levels

There has been extensive news coverage about 'soft option' A levels (see *The Times* 22/2/08) which describes research into the comparability of an A and an E grade in different subjects. It has been suggested by some that it is easier to get an A in some subjects than in others. In response to this, Cambridge has put together a list of A-level subjects that they consider to be less rigorous and would therefore probably only include them in an offer as a third subject. See www.cam.ac.uk/admissions/undergraduate/requirements/index.html or www.admissions.ox.ac.uk/vocationalqualifications for more information. However, I would advise that if you are set on doing an 'unacceptable' A level for some reason, make sure it is your fourth A level and do not do more than one.

List of 'unacceptable' A levels

- Accounting
- Art and Design (may be acceptable in some cases – check Architecture requirements, also this varies between colleges: some colleges accept Art as an academic A level and some do not, of course for Fine Art at Oxford it is acceptable)
- Business Studies
- Communication Studies
- Critical Thinking (as a fourth A level only)
- Dance
- Design and Technology (may be acceptable in some cases – check Engineering requirements)
- Drama/Theatre Studies (may be acceptable in some cases – check Education and English requirements (Cambridge only))
- Film Studies
- General Studies (as a fourth A level only)
- Health and Social Care
- Home Economics
- Information and Communication Technology
- Leisure Studies
- Media Studies
- Music Technology
- Performance Studies
- Performing Arts
- Photography
- Physical Education
- Sports Studies
- Travel and Tourism

Straight from the horse's mouth

To be a realistic applicant, a student will normally need to be offering two traditional academic subjects (i.e. two subjects not on the 'unacceptable list') . . . For students studying for the International Baccalaureate not more than one of the subjects listed should be taken a higher level to count as part of the Diploma.

Cambridge Admissions web pages

You are going to need to be predicted or get three or four As at A level. Due to the competitive nature of A level now, it is not enough to get 3 or 4 As at the end, you need to get 90% in the majority of the individual modules that make up the AS and A2. Also be aware that in 2010, A*s for A level are going to be introduced to differentiate the best from the good which will mean that you need to work extra hard to secure your A*s.

Straight from the horse's mouth

The admissions office will assess what the A* for A level means, when it comes into effect, and will probably request it in the most relevant subject.

Admissions Tutor, Cambridge

The degree of flexibility of your A level subject choice will depend to an extent to which course you apply. For example, if you are going to apply for Medicine at Cambridge then you will need three and a half A-levels in chemistry, physics, maths and biology (chemistry must be a full A-level). Although some subjects require specific subjects to be taken, some courses require no specific A-levels, just A grades in them and a proven interest in the subject to be studied at university. It is important that you can justify your subject choice and that the choice seems coherent. You need to make sure that you come across as a student who plans things carefully.

When looking at your A-level choices we ask ourselves whether the student has the intellectual and academic training to get through the first part of the Tripos.

Admissions Tutor, Cambridge

Subjects that do not require a specific A-level subject:

- Anglo-Saxon, Norse and Celtic
- Archaeology and Anthropology
- Classical Archaeology and Ancient History
- Classics four years (Cambridge) Law
- Geography (Cambridge) – at Oxford they do want Geography A level

- History of Art
- Human Sciences
- Land Economy (Cambridge)
- Law
- Oriental Sciences
- Philosophy (Cambridge)
- Philosophy and Theology
- PPE (Philosophy, Politics and Economics) (Oxford)
- SPS (Social and Political Sciences) (Cambridge)
- Theology.

If you have little idea about what you want to study at this stage, I would recommend studying the subjects you can get As in and also enjoy. If you are mathematically able, Maths is always a good bet as it can increase your options of subjects you can apply for at university. Similarly choosing an essay-writing based subject such as History or English is a good idea. If you want to take a science, Chemistry is the science that links together all the other sciences and will form a solid basis for many degrees, particularly in conjunction with Maths. In addition, languages are always an asset for jobs as well as for university. If you are weighing up two options of courses make sure you are taking the required subjects for both if possible. In the worst case scenario, if you realise you have chosen the wrong subject, you could sit the A level the next year at a tutorial college or buy the books, read round the subject and try learning it to yourself.

How many A levels?

Straight from the horse's mouth

Cambridge would prefer applicants thinking of stretching themselves, having chosen a coherent set of A-levels to do so by stretching themselves vertically by taking one or two Advanced Extension Awards rather than horizontally by taking a further A level.

Director of Admissions, Cambridge Colleges

It is much better to show 'broader and deeper knowledge of their chosen subject (or those closest to it if a new subject)':

If you are doing a science subject or Economics then you should consider doing Further Maths AS or A level as a fourth A level. Further Maths should not be a third A level. If you are doing [a degree in] biological sciences then do all the sciences and maths.

Chairman of the Admissions Forum, Cambridge

■ Tips for getting those As: revision and hard work

A levels are very different now from what they used to be. You are probably taking exams in the January and June of both your A-level years. This means that you need to be on top of your work and revision at all times. In order to achieve the highest grades you must work very hard constantly. This means going to see your teacher in your break if you did not understand the work in class. When revising for your A-level modules, I would advise buying some A-level study guides. Go to a bookshop or your local library and browse their school section. Pick a subject you know well such as Organic Chemistry and see how the book explains it. If it explains it well then it may well explain other topics well. I would recommend buying two different study guides per subject so that if you cannot follow one, you can use the other to get a different perspective. Many study guides have past exam questions which you can attempt and check the answers in the back. If you get an answer wrong then go back to the question and see if you can work it out. If you are really stumped then take the question to your teacher. Your teacher will be delighted that you are taking your studies seriously so do not worry about bombarding him/her with questions! The key is to show him/her that you have tried the question twice.

At A level it is often important to learn definitions or chains of events. Write them out and compare them with the definition in the textbook or study guide until you can do it perfectly. One would hope that your teachers are giving you lots of past paper practice and are letting you see the mark schemes. It is important to look at the mark schemes as it enables you to see directly what the examiner is looking for. If your teacher is not giving you many papers then ask him/her. Increasingly the exam boards are putting past papers and mark schemes on the internet. For example, for OCR, go to www.ocr.org.uk/pastpapermaterials. For other exam boards type their name into a search engine such as Google, select the qualification you are studying for and navigate to the past paper materials. It is also important to make sure you know what information you are meant to learn. Your teacher may have given you a copy of the syllabus – if not it can be downloaded on the Exam board's website – it is referred to as the 'specification'. Check the exam code with your teacher first in case there is more than one specification.

As you get nearer the exams, you will have to make sure that in addition to your usual study routine, you factor in revision time for after you come home from school. I suggest making a revision timetable for the two-month run-up to the exams listing every day you have until the exams including weekends so that you can plan your revision.

After school, when you have done your homework you should spend two hours doing revision. The most important thing is to make sure your revision is effective. Staring into space for two hours does not count as revision. At the end of each evening arrange the books ready for the next evening so that when you begin your revision session fresh and awake you do not have to waste valuable time sorting out where your books are.

Revision technique is a personal thing and you have probably already got plenty of ideas of how you work best if you have done well in your GCSEs. The key point is that in some subjects you need to learn lots of information. Reading the information through is not enough – you need to do something active with it. Try rewriting it in bullet point form or in a flow chart. Cover up the bullet points and try writing it again by heart. Draw out diagrams without looking at the original and then compare them with the original. Highlight any mistakes and draw them out again. Write out equations or reactions. Attempt a maths question for which you have a model answer, compare your stages of answers with theirs and see where you went wrong. Do the question again until you get it right.

Go and make a cup of tea after 50 minutes. This is your break – do not be tempted to start watching TV or going on MSN. Go back up to your study room and continue. When you do your next revision session, start by drawing out the diagrams and flow charts from the previous session without looking at your notes. You should be building up a bank of diagrams and flowcharts. You could put these on cards or just make your own notebook to refer to on the day of the exams – this should be a very concise summary.

It is important when you do your two hours of revision that your mobile phone is switched off and you are not on MSN. Two hours of emailing does not count as two hours of revision. There is an equation which no one ever tells you, which is 'work in = work out'. If you put in the work now then you will reap the rewards later. The important thing to get into your head is that you will not have much of a social life whilst you are revising. But do not worry, this is a temporary stage in your life and it is a means to an end. If you get those grades and get to a good university, hopefully Oxford or Cambridge, then your social life will be great when you get there.

When you know the dates and times of your exams, draw up a timetable and pin it on your wall. Make sure you write down how long each exam is, how many questions there are and based on the marks allocated to each section, how long each section should take you. Your teacher should be able to help you on this. It is important to make sure you have sorted out this basic strategy well in advance of your exam.

◼ Stress

All this revision can easily become stressful, so it is important to listen to your feelings. If you are exhausted then the best thing you can do is go to bed or perhaps take a day off from studying on the weekend. There are many effects of stress which include sleeplessness and headaches, tearfulness, loneliness, excessive eating or not eating enough. If you feel that you are suffering from these or similar symptoms then try talking to a friend or your parents about it. It may be that they can offer you some perspective. Perhaps you have a school counsellor you can see or if not go and see your GP. Studying for A levels is hard and many students are in a similar position.

Some practical measures you can take if you are feeling stressed or feel unable to get down to work are to change your work routine, maybe you would prefer to do your two hours of studying before school and not at night. Perhaps you would benefit from studying with a friend once in a while. Studying is an isolating process and it is important to build social activities into your timetable to keep yourself sane. Make sure you are partaking in some form of exercise regularly and are eating balanced and healthy meals. Don't eat while you study. It is distracting and you need to focus entirely on the work at hand.

■ Checklist

Have you understood?

- [ ] You will have to work very hard to secure As in all of your A levels.
- [ ] Some A levels are not worth as much as others.
- [ ] You have to be able to come up with some logic as to why you chose the A levels you did.

Follow it up

- [ ] Have you checked the A-level subject requirements for your course(s)?

03 Preparing to apply

The first step is to jot down on a piece of paper all the things of note you have done in recent years. Perhaps you have travelled to interesting countries, volunteered for an organisation, undertaken some work experience, attended some lectures about your subject or have gone to a summer school. Here are some questions that you may like to consider:

- What or who made you become interested in your subject?
- How can you demonstrate that you have followed up your interest?
- Have you read any interesting books?
- How can you demonstrate that you are able to commit to something (the admissions tutor will want evidence that you have enough tenacity to stick at the course and that you will be an asset to the college), for example, volunteering, work experience etc.
- Have you taken part in activities in your school, for example, debating, school newspaper, drama, choir or set up a society/club?

It is important to realise that to a certain extent some of these answers can be manufactured. For example, you may not have read any books about your subject, but you may still know you are interested in it. This is not good enough for the admissions tutor. You need to read some books. Ask your subject teacher for some suggestions. You need to find out where lectures about your subject are happening. Contact some of the well-known universities near you and ask for a list of lectures that are open to the public. You need to book yourself a place although they are free.

You also may not have had any work experience. It is very important to get some work experience not only to show commitment for the purposes of the UCAS form (i.e. if you are committed enough to hold down a job and do well at it, you will also be committed enough to finish your degree and get the most out of it) but also because it is very helpful later on in life when you are deciding what sort of job you would like to do. For example, you may get work experience in some kind of office and realise that office work is not for you. You may shadow a barrister and think that you can see yourself doing that as a career. Getting work experience can sometimes be tricky and you have to implement several strategies at the same time. This includes asking all your relatives and getting your parents to ask their friends if you can go to work with them for a week or more;

asking your school if they have links with your local community and whether they can set up some work experience, you can also visit your local Connexions Office which is a government run organisation that helps young people make career decisions and you can also write/email or telephone organisations directly and ask if you can get some work experience or volunteer. The organisation may ask for a reference from your teacher and you will have to ask them if they are happy to write a reference for you. Perhaps it is becoming clear that your teacher takes a very important role in your university application – not only directly in terms of writing your university reference but also indirectly, as they will write your reference for work experience, if necessary, which is important for your Personal Statement.

Organising work experience or volunteering can take several weeks or months so make sure you do this well in advance of your AS level summer. Remember, any type of work experience is fine.

Straight from the horse's mouth

What you gain from the work experience is more valuable than the actual work experience.

It can be just as valuable making tea in a hospice as shadowing a consultant in a top hospital.

It shows just as much commitment working every Saturday in a supermarket as being an Olympic swimmer.

Admissions Tutor, Cambridge

I encourage my students at the beginning of their AS year to write their 'dream' Personal Statement. This means you need to describe the work experience you want to undertake and what you think you may learn from it. It will be obvious where you have gaps and where you need to take some initiative to fill in those gaps such as organising work experience, getting involved in extra-curricular activities or reading widely around your subject.

■ Getting work experience

Below is a sample letter you could send to gain some work experience. The words in italics need to be adapted as appropriate for your situation. There are some important points to note.

1| When you write a letter, if you know the name of the person to whom it is addressed you must sign off 'Yours sincerely', if you do not know the name of the person and you write 'Dear

Sir/Madam' or 'To whom it may concern', then you must sign off 'Yours faithfully'.

2| It is much better to write the person's name rather than write a generic 'To whom it may concern' so make a phone call and find out who deals with work experience or who the Human Resources Manager is. If you are writing a letter to a contact, then address the letter directly to them.

3| Whether you ask for work experience or to shadow someone depends on their profession. If they are a barrister or a doctor it would be best to shadow them, which means following them throughout the week and attending everything they attend. If you are applying to work in a business then you should ask for work experience as you could be given a project to do and really demonstrate your skills (which you can then write about in your Personal Statement!).

4| It is important to organise your work experience well in advance (at least three months) as businesses and organisations are inundated with requests for work experience.

5| The 'Enc. CV' at the bottom lets the reader know that as well as the letter you have enclosed a document, in this case your CV.

6| Your school should help you write your CV and there are many books and websites around to help you. As a quick guide I have included a sample CV.

7| It is much more efficient to email your work experience letter and CV. When you call up the business or organisation ask if they have an email address you can send it to. If you do send it in email form you do not need to write your address, their address or the date. Just start 'Dear Mr Bloggs'.

8| If you do not hear back after four days, you need to ring them up and explain that you sent them a letter about work experience and have not heard anything and see what they have to say.

9| You need to apply for lots of work experience as not every organisation offers these opportunities and places will be limited. The more you apply for, the greater your chances of getting a good placement, or possibly even two. If you do get offered two placements, do them both. The more varied experiences you have the more you have to write about.

10| On the last day of your work experience, hand in a thank you letter, using the model letter below and ask if they are happy to write a reference to send to your teacher both in the letter and verbally. This is crucial as your teacher can incorporate comments in their reference about you. The more you help your teacher out the better the reference will be. An example of a reference from an employer is given on the next page.

■ Sample letter requesting work experience placement

Mr Joe Bloggs MP The House of Commons Westminster London SW1	Your address Your telephone number Your email address

Date

Dear Mr Bloggs,

I would very much like to *undertake some work experience in your office/shadow you for a week* because I am very interested in exploring a career as a *barrister*. I am currently studying for my A levels in *Spanish, Maths and Chemistry* at *Green Fields* School and I have *enclosed/attached* my CV. My summer holiday commences on *July 14 and continues until August 16*. I very much hope that you will be able to fit a week in sometime between those dates. Please could you contact me at the address or email above at your convenience.

I look forward to hearing from you.

Yours sincerely,

Your signature

Your name

Enc. CV

Straight from the horse's mouth

I wanted to get some work experience in the media business but had no contacts. I wrote letters to fifteen organisations 'cold'. Ten never got back to me, four were unable to take me on as they had other work experience students and one offered me a week's work experience. I would definitely apply to many organisations at the same time.

Oxford Applicant

■ Sample thank you letter

Mr Joe Bloggs MP The House of Commons Westminster London SW1	Your address Your telephone number Your email address

Date

Dear Mr Bloggs,

Thank you so much for showing me around the House of Commons on Tuesday, and for letting me work in your office this week. I really enjoyed it – especially being allowed to watch the House of Commons debate. I was wondering if you would be so kind as to write a reference about me and send it to my teacher at Green Fields School, Ealing London, WO OAA.

Thank you very much again.

Yours sincerely,

Your signature

Your name

◼ Model Curriculum Vitae (CV)

At this stage of your life, you may feel that there is little to write on your CV. However, the CV is a useful document to enclose with your work experience letter as it gives the employer some useful basic information and the final section of 'interests and activities' adds a bit of colour.

The format of CVs varies considerably but a general rule of thumb is that they must not exceed two A4 pages in length, they must be word processed and not handwritten and they must be easy on the eye to read. To that end, I favour the model below, which includes a summary box at the top which succinctly says who you are and what work experience you are looking for.

You must be able to back up anything you write on your CV, just like your Personal Statement. Put down any work experience you have, including babysitting, as the new employer may want some form of reference for you. If you have absolutely no work experience, you could ask your teacher to write a reference for you. You should constantly update your CV. When you have some work experience under your belt, remember to add it to your CV as well as using it in your Personal Statement. You will find that when you come to apply for jobs after university, your work experience will still be very useful. These model letters can be used when you are applying for internships in your summer vacations too!

Example CV

Curriculum Vitae

Josephine Bloggs

A-level student, interested in studying Chemistry at university and pursuing a career in patent law

(Continued)

Your address

Nationality: *British*
Date of Birth: *7 February 1990*
Tel: *01865 777 777*
Mobile: *07765 123 456*
Email: myemail@email.com

EDUCATION

Secondary: Green Fields School, London (2001–2008)
3 A Levels: Spanish, Chemistry, Maths
Grades pending

10 GCSE'S: French, Latin, Spanish, Dual Award Science, English Language, English Literature, History, Computer Studies – All grade A*; Maths – Grade A

SKILLS

Presentation

- Can explain ideas clearly and concisely (presentations at school)
- Excellent public speaking skills (debated competitively for school)
- Inter-personal skills
- Negotiation and organisational skills (founded and chaired charity committee)

Analysis

- Won prize for ICT GCSE project write-up which tested a system I devised

Research and writing

- Commended for research and writing skills in Spanish essay

Computation

- Skilled in Microsoft Word, Excel, Internet Explorer, Power Point, and in using interactive whiteboards

WORK EXPERIENCE

Babysitting   July 2007
Newspaper round, Green Field   January 2006–January 2007
  newsagent, London

INTERESTS AND ACTIVITIES

- Part of the netball team
- Enjoy cooking
- Enjoy going to the theatre

Checklist

Have you understood?

☐ You have to start doing some activities to prove you are interested in your subject.

☐ Work experience may take several months to organise and you have to persevere.

Follow it up

☐ If you are applying to Oxbridge in a year's time, have you written to 15 organisations asking for work experience?

☐ Have you started a log book?

04 References

At a college in Cambridge, there were 90 applicants for six places to read Economics. Eighteen were deselected (rejected) on the basis of their UCAS forms. There are three reasons for this:

1| GCSEs and predicted A-level grades were not good enough.
2| The school's reference was bad.
3| The Personal Statement was bad.

The next two chapters will focus on References and the Personal Statement.

Your teacher will probably have to write many references. How can you help her (and thus help yourself) to write a good reference? The first thing you can do is to make sure that you have regular contact with your teacher. Make sure they know who you are and how nice you are. Are you someone who has a 100% attendance rate and whose teachers never have a complaint about? Have you discussed your application with your teacher? Do they know the things that you have accomplished lower down the school? Are they aware of your proudest achievements?

There are two practical measures I would take. First, ask the person you shadowed or the employer where you did your work experience (or your employer of your Saturday job) to write you a reference and have it sent directly to your teacher. Don't be afraid to ask. Most employers are more than happy to do this for someone who has impressed them during their work experience placement or weekend job. This will mean that your teacher will see that you have been proactive and it will also give your teacher an easy way to start your application.

Here are two example references that students may have got after doing some work experience. Can you see why they would be helpful to your teacher? What sort of qualities could your teacher pick out about you from them? N.B. You may request to see any reference written about you.

■ How to interact with this section of the book

This section of the book has space for you to write your comments. In order to learn the most from this section of the book it is important for you to do these close reading exercises (it is also good practice for your Oxford and Cambridge interview!). When you read the sections of text, it is important to underline and put question marks next to various points to come back to or to question and jot down your overall impressions in the space provided. I always tell my students that it is possible to do 'active reading' only with a pen in your hand.

■ Example of an employer reference from shadowing a professional

Georgina spent a week with us at the National Hospital for Neurology on a work placement. During that time she closely observed the work of physicians, surgeons and nurses as they cared for people whilst inpatients and outpatients. Georgina is clearly committed to a career in medicine and has an advanced and realistic understanding of its demands. Our impression was that Georgina as well as being very academic has excellent empathetic and social skills. She was very enthusiastic about the time she spent with us and will make an excellent doctor. She was at all times punctual and reliable and her pleasant manner both with staff and patients was of specific note. Her interest, enthusiasm and intelligence bode well for her as she follows her desired path of interest in medicine. I have no hesitation in recommending her for placement in medical school.

■ Example of an employer reference from volunteering over a sustained period of time

Georgina has volunteered at the Hospice for a year and is a most valuable member of the team of volunteers. She is dedicated and committed, doing regular shifts here. Georgina has been very dependable and reliable, proving that she can handle awkward and sometimes potentially upsetting situations with great tact and maturity.

Despite having a busy study schedule Georgina has volunteered her own precious spare time at weekends – and given invaluable service to the Hospice. It is always a pleasure to see her and her enthusiasm is infectious.

Georgina is very popular with members of staff and other volunteers alike. Patients, who in many instances are extremely ill, especially appreciate seeing a friendly and familiar face.

Your comments:

My comments:

For Medicine, it is important to say that the student has interpersonal skills and can work as part of a team. However, every referee knows that and will write it for their student. It is much more impressive to the university for the teacher to have some evidence of these skills and be able to quote a work experience reference directly. This also has the added benefit of telling the university that you have done several types of work experience, which helps to give evidence of your interest in your subject. You can see why it is important to make a good impression on your employer and how your teacher can use the information in the reference.

Here follows a reference that I wrote for a student applying to read Economics at Cambridge. Can you unpick the reference and list all the things Adam (not his real name) has attended that are evidence of the fact that he has a genuine interest in Economics outside of the classroom?

■ Reference for Adam Smith

Adam Smith joined Green Field School in September 2007. He has been predicted four As in Economics, Physics, Maths and Politics and will take up Further Maths in January. He will also take an AEA in Economics.

Adam is a boy of exceptional ability and would be an asset to any university that he joined. He has developed an enormous capacity for self-study, as illustrated by his prolific reading above and beyond any A-level syllabus. He has shown extraordinary initiative in submitting an article to *The Economist* about the recent Conservative Party's publication 'The UK Economic Competitiveness Report'. He showed me the article which exhibits university-level skills of critical analysis and an extremely mature perspective and awareness of events in the wider world.

The Head of Economics describes Adam as being able to grasp abstract concepts and theories with considerable ease and that his desire to use these tools in a process of application, analysis and evaluation is first rate. He is very stimulating to teach and constantly asks searching questions on current issues. Adam is a highly organised and disciplined student. He has particularly good problem solving skills. In the classroom, he is more than keen to have in-depth discussions which bodes well for seminar and tutorial work. He also achieved 'Honour Roll' at his school in Costa Rica as recognition of his dedication, critical thinking, responsible action and intelligence.

Adam has undertaken some work experience in the finance/accounting department of a corporate travel agency in Costa Rica. He learnt how to balance the books and other specific accounting procedures. The reference from the Head of Finance of the company describes Adam's work as outstanding and explains that 'despite his inexperience, his work ethic and the quality of his work was brilliant'.

Adam used to take part in the school's Investment Club, where they 'traded' FTSE 100 shares using real daily prices from the newspaper. A competition was held to see which group could make the most profit from their investments. Adam demonstrated considerable leadership skills in his group. He was also awarded an 'Honorary Mention' for his outstanding participation in the ASEAN Regional Forum Model United Nations.

Adam is a lively and sociable young man. He is also a talented actor, as attested by the Certificate of Merit he was awarded in March 2007 in the Competitive Arts Festival. Furthermore, Adam was an active and committed participant in Speech and Drama at school where he performed in *The Glass Menagerie, Othello* and other plays.

We wholeheartedly commend Adam to the universities for which he is applying and are certain that he will make an excellent contribution.

> **Your comments:**

My comments:

You should have a fairly long list of Adam's extracurricular activities. It is your teacher's job to write that list in reference form and extract the qualities about you from them. You should ask your teacher if it would be helpful for them for you to write a list of the things you have done. If they know you well they may feel this is unnecessary but most teachers will welcome a list. It is up to them to weave into the list a narrative about you but in order for them to write positive comments you will need to start cultivating a positive relationship with them as soon as you can.

On the extra Oxford form and in a supplementary letter that your teacher can send with your application (discussed later), your teacher can make a further comment about you if she feels she has something to add specific to your Oxbridge application (the UCAS reference is for all your universities not just Oxford or Cambridge). There may be no need to write anything else.

Here is an example of an additional reference that I felt was necessary to write for Adam:

I am aware that your college requires an average of 90% at AS Maths and Adam's average as it stands is 82%. However, Adam has gone from strength to strength in his Maths and has impressed us all with achieving As in all of his mock exam papers and specifically achieving 96% in his most recent test. We have absolutely no doubt as to his aptitude in Maths and his disappointing AS Mechanics result was due to the unfortunate circumstances mentioned in the Special Access Scheme form and in no way reflects his ability. Adam is an extremely well-rounded and talented individual and in addition to the UCAS reference I would like to mention that he is fluent in Spanish.

The Special Access Scheme (Cambridge only) that is mentioned guarantees you an interview at Cambridge if your grades have been affected by family circumstances or health reasons or if you come from an atypical Cambridge background. See www.cam.ac.uk/admissions/undergraduate/apply/#csas for more information. I did not feel it was necessary to write an extra reference for the following student who applied to Cambridge to read Medicine. Read the reference and this time write a list of the sort of things, in general, a teacher may put in a reference.

■ Reference for Helena Jones

Helena Jones joined Green Fields School in September 2007, having changed direction in her career choice. She originally decided to study Politics, and achieved A grades in English, German and Religious Studies at A level and A grades in Chemistry and History at A/S. During her gap year she decided that she would read Medicine and to that end enrolled on Chemistry and Biology A-level courses here at Green Fields School.

Helena has been predicted Grade A in A-level Chemistry and Biology and will start Maths AS in January 2008. As she is such a strong candidate we predict that she will get an A in this subject as well. She is earnest and focussed in class and is able to solve problems on her own carefully, with little assistance. Her written work has been of a very high standard showing that she can construct concise, well-phrased explanations. She interacts with the groups in all of her classes, demonstrating that she is both a good listener and not afraid to voice her opinion. All her teachers believe that she is a delight to teach.

Helena has demonstrated considerable initiative particularly in how she organised her own work experience at Nottingham Hospital and at her local General Practice. It was noted how well Helena interacted with the patients and staff and her punctuality and reliability were exemplary. She is very keen to ask questions to further her understanding.

She is an all-rounder who, as can be seen from her grades and varied subject choices, excels at many different combinations of subjects and is notable for her ability to balance a very full academic schedule with a very broad range of extracurricular activities. At her previous school she took part in debating to a very high level and was commended for her speech about AIDS at the European Youth Parliament in 2006. She took an active role in Young Enterprise, the Model United Nations and organised the Amnesty International letter writing club. This year, she is working for an NGO and for a hospice in her free time.

Helena was elected Deputy Head Girl by her peers at her previous school and fulfilled the demanding range of duties this required very conscientiously and diplomatically. She has a very highly developed sense of responsibility and duty to those around her and beyond. Her gap year projects have shown that she has a very strong social conscience and awareness of issues beyond her immediate environment.

Helena is a quite outstanding student as her excellent A level and AS level results attest. She shows herself to be curious, innovative and self-reliant in her studies and is able to apply her intellect to all that she does.

We wholeheartedly commend her to the universities for which she is applying and are certain that she will make an excellent contribution.

> **Your comments:**

My comments:

You should have compiled a list of the sorts of things that go into a reference. Your next step is to make sure that you are doing those things – have you done some work experience, have you read around your subject and, most importantly, does your teacher know about it?

What happens if you think that for some reason your teacher will be writing you a bad reference?

If you feel that you do not have a good relationship with your teacher and the reference they write may put you at a disadvantage, go to speak to the Deputy Head or Head about your concerns and ask if another teacher would write it for you instead.

■ Checklist

Have you understood?

☐ You need to start cultivating a good relationship with the person who is going to write your reference with you early on. They are not allowed to write you a 'bad' reference as theoretically you could sue for defamation, but there are ways of writing a bad reference that admissions tutors will pick up on. Writing a reference of a few words without waxing lyrical about any particular quality has a subtext that says 'bad student'.

Follow it up

☐ Ask your teacher if they would like a list of the activities you have done.

☐ Have your work experience employer send a reference directly to your teacher (and it does no harm to ask for a copy to be sent to you as well).

05 The application

This chapter is going to focus on the nuts and bolts of the application forms. I am sure you have heard of the Personal Statement, which is part of the application form, and this shall be treated in some depth later on in the chapter. In fact, the first draft of the Personal Statement should be written several months before you fill out the forms.

■ The UCAS form

UCAS is the University and Colleges Admissions Service and is the central way that you have to apply to university. Your UCAS form, when complete, will be emailed to your five chosen universities. They all see exactly the same form so it is important that you do not write anything specific about one university because the other universities will think that you don't want to go to their university and will not offer you a place.

In September you will have to log on to the UCAS website and register. Go to www.ucas.com/students/apply. In order to do this you will need an email address. If you haven't got one go to yahoo.com or hotmail.com and get a free one. When you register you will be sent an application number, user name and password which you will need every time you log on to UCAS.

The entire application is done online. You can fill in the UCAS form in stages. There are several sections:

Personal details, which include your name, address and date of birth.

Student support, which is where you have to select your fee code. If you are a British national your local authority will be your fee payer. That is not to say that you won't have to pay less, but substantially less than a student from outside the EU.

Next is an **Additional information** section in which you can write 'Activities in preparation for Higher Education'. These activities specifically refer to attending summer schools in preparation for university either run by the universities themselves or by trusts such as the Sutton Trust. See www.suttontrust.com/index.asp or contact UCAS for more information (www.ucas.com/about_us/contact_us).

Now we get onto the nitty gritty of the form – the university choices. You can only apply to one of Oxford or Cambridge. Choose the correct university code from the drop-down menu (CAM C05 for Cambridge and OXF 033 for Oxford). You also need to write what UCAS calls the 'campus code', which is in fact the college code. A drop-down list will appear. You will also need to choose the subject and select which year of entry you are applying (i.e. do you intend to take a gap year?).

The next section is very important – **education**. You need to write down every GCSE and A level (or equivalent qualification) and grade you have taken under the heading of the school in which you took them. If you are applying post-A level you need to write down all of your modules grades. It would be helpful to amass all your GCSE and A-level module certificates before you begin this section of the application form to aid the efficient completion of this section.

The next section is **Employment**. This is not the same as work experience although both paid employment and work experience can be discussed in your Personal Statement. This is about jobs you have been paid to do. It doesn't matter how insignificant it sounds to you – write it down. Admissions tutors will be pleased to see that you have had the commitment and maturity to hold down a job, even if it's a paper round.

Next is the Personal Statement – your chance to show the admissions tutors how you write and how informed you are about your subject. More on this later. You should write this in a Word document, spell check it and read it through carefully and when ready copy and paste it into the UCAS form.

The next stage is to send the form off (it goes to your teacher). In order to do this, you have to pay £17 (for the 2008/9 cycle) to UCAS for processing by credit card (your school may have a policy of paying this for you so you need to check before you part with any money). Your teacher will then be able to open it on the teachers' part of the UCAS site. They will read it to check everything is correct and will then write their reference and predicted grades. Then they will send it off and the universities will get it immediately.

For Oxford and Cambridge all of this has to happen by 15 October. Your teacher may need some time to write the reference so I would have this all done and sent to her two weeks before this date.

However, that is not all. Oxford requires another form to be filled out. As of September 2008, Cambridge will require a Supplementary Application Questionnaire (SAQ) to be filled out (in line with other universities). The SAQ will be online and will cost nothing to send. The Oxford form is a paper form and it needs to be sent to Oxford by 15 October. Again, it needs your teacher's input so fill it out well before this date. You need to send £10 with the Oxford form as they charge a processing fee.

For both the Oxford application forms there is a space to write an 'additional Personal Statement'. This is where you could write a reason why you think you are particularly suited to their course, which you could not have written on your Personal Statement that gets sent to all the universities. You also need to give a breakdown of all your A-level module grades. For Oxford and Cambridge the end A-level grade is sometimes not enough for highly competitive subjects, they may stipulate that you have to get over 90% in each of your modules. Your teacher can also write an additional reference if there is something that needs to be said that is particularly relevant to Oxford or Cambridge but this is not always necessary (see chapter 4 on reference). There is a different form to fill in if you are a mature student or want to apply for a choral/organ award but this should be made clear on the Oxford and Cambridge admissions websites.

If you are applying for Law or Medicine at either university you have to apply online well before 15 October to take a special exam called the LNAT (for Law) or the BMAT (for Medicine). You will be emailed a reference number and you need to enter this reference number on your UCAS form. This and the other written exams are the subject of the next chapter. In addition you may need to send some written work. There is a separate cover sheet for this and your school should give it to you. You can also download it from the admissions website. As usual, if in doubt call the admissions office.

Straight from the horse's mouth

The submitted essay is often used as the starting point for discussion in the interview. The essay can show us whether the candidate has the ability to argue and has academic confidence. One student submitted an essay that his teacher marked as a grade B minus, but he was confident of his work and we valued his confidence.

Admissions Tutor, Cambridge

■ What qualities are Oxford and Cambridge looking for?

Let us step back and consider the qualities for which Oxford and Cambridge are looking.

They want to know that you:

1| Have an ability and readiness to join in discussion of the subject
2| Have an understanding and commitment to the subject
3| Know major developments in subject
4| Know why you want to study it
5| Know what the course at Oxford or Cambridge entails and that you are suited to it.

Straight from the horse's mouth

We look for whether the candidates show stamina, independence, ambition, commitment and organisational skills in order to assess whether they can survive the intense and pressured atmosphere that is Cambridge.

Admissions Tutor, Cambridge

A successful applicant will be:

- *Well-informed and very keen to learn more*
- *Not satisfied with the status quo of their knowledge*
- *Determined to get to the bottom of any question put in front of them*
- *Must be a pleasure to teach on a one-to-one basis a couple of hours a week*
- *Will make the most contribution to the college in academic terms.*

Admissions Tutor, Cambridge

How can you demonstrate these things and in which document (reference, Personal Statement, 'extra Personal Statement', submitted work or interview) do you think they will appear?

1| Have an ability and readiness to join in discussion of the subject

Your subject teachers will make a comment to the teacher who writes the reference as to how much you participate in the class. Make sure you start doing this. I think this quality is evidenced in your reference.

2| Have an understanding and commitment to the subject

You need to have read around your subject – ask your teacher for a book list or go to the faculty website for Oxford or Cambridge for your subject, download the first year reading list and pick a few books. If in doubt, speak to the admissions tutor directly.

You need to demonstrate a sustained commitment to your subject. Can you prove that your interest in your subject has been growing over a long time? Have you gone to conferences and lectures?

I think this quality is evidenced in your Personal Statement.

3| Know major developments in the subject

You nee d to keep abreast of current affairs in your field and in general. Start keeping a current affairs diary. Each day go to the BBC news website (http://news.bbc.co.uk . . . .) or read a quality newspaper (*Telegraph, Independent, The Times* etc.) and write down five headlines in your diary. To keep abreast of current affairs in your field you can click on the type of news, for example, science or health on the BBC news website. There are also specialist journals you should be reading regularly such as the *New Scientist* or *The Economist*. Ask your teacher what journal they can recommend. Subject specific headlines also need to be noted in your diary. Before your interview you need to reread your current affairs diary.

I think this quality can be evidenced most strongly in your interview but the fact that you keep up to date with current events in your field and beyond can be mentioned in your Personal Statement. Your teacher can also mention it in the reference.

4| Know why you want to study it

You will most certainly be asked this at interview and you need to explain the reasons clearly in your Personal Statement. Just like with your A-level choice, you need to make sure that your choice of course sounds informed and planned. Be prepared to tell the story as to how you became interested in the subject and what you may intend to do with it.

5| Know what the course at Oxford or Cambridge entails and that you are suited to it

You need to have read the course description thoroughly and be able to explain what you will study in each year. The course web pages will explain this in depth. The course at Oxford or Cambridge is often very different from that at other universities. Clearly, your UCAS Personal Statement is not the place to extol the virtues of Oxford and Cambridge as the other universities will see it too. The place to demonstrate that you know what the course entails is the 'extra Personal Statement' and in your interview.

■ Checklist

Have you understood?

☐ There are two applications that you need to make in order to apply to Oxford and Cambridge.

☐ The UCAS form is completed online (£15). The extra Oxford form is done on paper (and costs £10). The Cambridge form is called the Supplementary Application Questionnaire is completed online (and is free).

☐ You can apply to up to five universities (four for Medicine or Dentistry) and although you do not need to apply for the same course for each one, practically the courses need to be similar to your Personal Statement, which is the section in the UCAS form of free text, describes why you want to do the course you want to do. Clearly, due to the fact that the same form goes to all your chosen universities you cannot be too specific about the courses or mention a specific university.

Follow it up

☐ Get all your GCSE and A-level module certificates together so that you can quickly write down all the information.

☐ Keep a current affairs diary.

☐ Get hold of the reading lists from the first year courses.

☐ Ask your teachers to recommend extra reading.

☐ Keep a log book of the lectures and other events you attend.

06 The Personal Statement

According to Cambridge, each applicant is assessed on six criteria to give a holistic view of the student:

- Academic record (GCSE and AS)
- School/college reference
- Personal Statement
- Submitted work where requested
- Test results
- Performance at interview.

(*Applying to Cambridge: Advice for teachers, Tutors and HE Advisers 2008 Entry.*)

However, some admissions tutors do not look too carefully at the Personal Statement and do not mention it at all in the interview. Others will pick specific bits from it and ask you to expand upon various points. The point is you have to be prepared. If you mention a book you enjoyed reading about your subject make sure you reread it and talk about it in detail. You need to be able to substantiate everything you say in your Personal Statement.

Straight from the horse's mouth

The Personal Statement is most likely to be the most difficult document a 17-year-old will have written – there are many complexities such as how to fine-tune the tone of the statement so that it is not too boastful but able to sell the student.

Admissions Tutor, Cambridge

The first point that it seems necessary to make is that the Personal Statement should be personal. I have known of a case where a student used a Personal Statement from his friend who applied to university five years earlier. UCAS now have a special system called the 'Similarity Detection Service' where they can trace if certain word combinations have been used before. If the computer finds a very close match then a letter is sent to all of your university choices and they are told that your statement has been copied from a previous applicant. At that point it is up to the universities to decide how to deal with the fraudulent student. It is fraud, by the way, as in the last part of the UCAS form you have to declare that everything on the form is true. Clearly Oxford or Cambridge will not bother to look at a candidate if it comes to their attention that the potential student has plagiarised somebody else's work.

Aside from the ethical dimension, plagiarism is an offence and taken very seriously at all universities.

What should go into a Personal Statement?

Straight from the horse's mouth

The subject-related content of the Personal Statement ought to take priority

An admissions tutor will read the Personal Statement asking themselves the following questions about the candidate:

- *Have they chosen the right subject for the right reasons?*
- *Can they survive in an intense and pressured atmosphere?*
- *Do they have a range of interests and aptitudes?*
- *Does the Personal Statement confirm their depth of interest in the subject?*
- *What has the candidate studied independently?*

Admissions Tutor, Cambridge

Perhaps the best way of answering this question is to consider the purpose of the Personal Statement. The first thing that Oxford and Cambridge will look at is whether you have been predicted three As. Let's assume you have. They will also want to see five or six glittering A*s at GCSE and a glowing reference from your teacher. It used to be the case that almost all applicants to Oxford and Cambridge got an interview and at that stage the best was differentiated from the second best. However, due to the sheer volume of applicants these days, Oxford and Cambridge cannot invite all applicants to interview. All things being equal, with two (or more) candidates having the same calibre of reference and the same examination grades, they will next turn to the Personal Statement to try to differentiate students. After selecting a certain number of candidates to interview, depending on the subject (see information in Chapter 7) they will ask the applicant to sit an exam before the interview. For some very oversubscribed subjects you can get 'deselected' (rejected) at this stage. You can also be deselected if your module scores are not high enough for some subjects. For example, if you have not got 90% in most of your Maths modules and you are applying for Engineering you may well be deselected. Finally you will be called to interview. The Personal Statement is also the place where you can explain what you intend to do in your gap year if applicable.

We can conclude that your Personal Statement will have to contain something that makes the interviewer want to meet you. You have to sound interesting and show that you are serious about studying your subject. Let's start by reading a section of a previous student's Personal Statement. My students have kindly let me use their Personal Statements but, a word of warning, do not copy any sentences – you will be found out and it is wrong! You will struggle in the interview if asked detailed questions about your Personal Statement if it is not true. When reading the section of the statement, underline or highlight any phrases or words that make you think that the student is interesting and keen to study their subject intensely (which is what happens at these universities). After reading the paragraph, jot down your comments. This is a useful exercise in itself as often minutes before your interview, you are asked to critically analyse an article or a piece of literature (depending on your subject) and you need to be able to come up with well argued comments. Adam (not his real name) applied to Cambridge to read Economics. He got an interview.

Straight from the horse's mouth

Applicants who are not invited for interview are unsuccessful because their academic track record, admission test performance (where appropriate) and school/college reference indicate that they have no realistic chance of winning a place, not because their Personal Statement let them down.

Director of Admissions, Cambridge Colleges

How long should a Personal Statement be?

There isn't a specific word limit as such but a space limit (47 lines) and a limit of 4,000 characters. I would advise you to write your draft Personal Statement on a computer and after you have revisited it several times you can copy and paste it into the UCAS form (which is online). For details about how to navigate your way through the UCAS form go to www.ucas.com. Forty-eight lines, as a rough guide, corresponds to about 700 words but it depends on how you divide up your paragraphs and whether you leave a line between paragraphs (it is up to you if you do this).

Adam's Personal Statement

Paragraph 1

Physics answers the question of why. Maths is a tool to solve quantitative issues. Politics is the study of the structure of law, government and policy. Economics, as I see it, is everything in between.

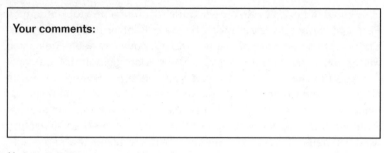

My comments:

The introduction needs to capture the admissions tutor's attention and make them want to read on. I think this introduction is punchy. It doesn't say that he doesn't enjoy the study of his other A levels but it explains why he thinks Economics is so good.

Paragraph 2

I thoroughly enjoy and am extremely interested in Economics. I believe that the distinct view on the world that economists have and the power to do good is why I am so enthused about the subject. I'm particularly drawn to Development Economics, but acknowledge the role that other spheres of Economics such as Econometrics, Micro and Macroeconomics play in the constitution of this field. This is why my current goal as a student of Economics is to learn as much about the subject in general. To this end, I have read several works of prominent economists. Delving into mind-expanding texts such as 'Development as Freedom', 'Capitalism and Freedom', 'Globalisation and its Discontents' and 'Wealth of Nations'. In addition to my individual exploration, I have attended courses at Harvard University and at Brown University for Economics and Global Development respectively.

Your comments:

My comments:

This paragraph has the effect of making me believe that Adam has a serious interest in Economics. He has identified a field of Economics that he is particularly drawn to. The danger of making such a comment is that he is giving the Admissions tutor ammunition – the admissions tutor may ask him detailed questions about Adam's understanding of Development Economics. This is not a bad thing, it just means he needs to be prepared to answer questions about this topic. Adam mentions several well-known books about Economics. However, he has not given the authors' names, which in my view is a mistake even though some of the books are very well known. I would have preferred to have seen Adam Smith's Wealth of Nations or Wealth of Nations by Adam Smith. This is because at university referencing works correctly becomes increasingly important. Attending university courses in a summer, or going to some sort of master class is an excellent way to show that you are really interested in studying the subject.

Paragraph 3

My passion for Economics, especially Development Economics, comes as a result of my background and experiences. I have been fortunate enough to travel, experience different cultures, lifestyles and perspectives. Seeing suffering and poverty, through community service and observation, has made me internalise these issues. Possessing a heritage that combines both economically developed and developing nations as I have lived in both Costa Rica and Britain has underlined this problem for me. Throughout my life, I have seen myself as a problem solver and I believe this has been highlighted through Young Enterprise.* Being Head of Production, I was in charge of overcoming difficulties such as rising costs. We did not win in the end, but it was a great learning experience and one that showed me the importance of thinking creatively.

Your comments:

My comments:

This paragraph cleverly manages to relay the fact that Adam has had an interesting life as he has lived in two very different countries and reinforces the fact that he is really interested in Economics. It also explains that he took part in extracurricular activities at school which shows that he was able to handle not only his A-level workload, but could take on extra responsibility. Being involved in Young Enterprise also demonstrates that Adam can work as a member of a team, which is an important quality that an admissions tutor may appreciate.

---

*Young Enterprise is a national competition where you can set up a business in a team when you are in Year 12 in order to gain experience of marketing, financial modelling and strategy. You are assessed on different facets of business and can win a prize for excellence in these fields and overall. Ask your teacher for more information.

Paragraph 4

I was selected to attend a Presidential Classroom programme in Washington DC and with great enthusiasm was able to debate and learn more in depth about the functioning of government and policy. I was also selected to represent my school in the University of Costa Rica's Law competition for schools which we won. That taught me the importance of different points of view and acknowledging them. Having to argue either for a multi-national corporation to construct an energy plant or for the preservation of the environment and the interests of the town affected by the construction.

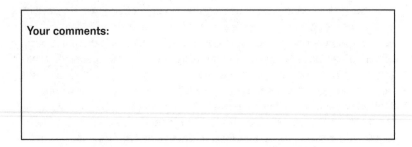

Your comments:

My comments:

This paragraph clearly shows that Adam has taken part in extracurricular activities. More than just list them, Adam has explained what he got out of them which shows that he thinks about his own development carefully.

Paragraph 5

Aside from travelling and learning, I appreciate the Arts and sports greatly. Acting is a passion of mine and started by attending Theatre Saturday School at the age of six. Since then I have been involved in different types of work, for instance, I was involved with a professional children's production which produced the play Annie and I played the lead male role. In the arena of sports, I am a keen footballer. I played for the 1st XI football team at my school.

Your comments:

My comments:

Most students put in a short paragraph detailing other extracurricular activities that do not relate to their academic subject. This helps give the impression that you are an all-rounder. This type of paragraph is less important than the others but at least a couple of lines should be there.

Closing sentence:

Economics has developed into my newest and greatest interest as it seems to combine not only all my academic endeavours but also permeates my pursuits out of the classroom.

Your comments:

My comments:

It is not necessary to have a closing sentence and sometimes they can sound a bit false. If you do feel a need to sum up then Adam's sentence is a good example.

Overall comments:

The element of the Personal Statement that is clearly lacking is any mention of work experience or volunteering. However, Adam has done many activities to demonstrate his interest in Economics.

Your comments:

Now you have critically analysed Adam's Personal Statement, you should have a go writing your first draft. You are going to be editing your draft many times and showing it to many people so it will not be perfect by any means. The way to write the best Personal Statement is to give yourself several weeks – maybe eight. I advise my students to write their first draft in their third term of their AS year. If you leave it for a couple of weeks and then come back to it, you will be sufficiently removed from it that you will be able to critically analyse your own work.

You need to get various people to read your draft of your Personal Statement. Ask your friends and family to read it and give them a pen so that they can read actively. Ask them if your Personal Statement gives a flavour of you, not only in terms of content but also in terms of writing style. It is very important that there are no spelling or grammatical mistakes as these stand out like a sore thumb and create a bad impression. Hopefully your friends and family will be able to spot these. When you have made or considered making the changes they suggest, give the Personal Statement to your teacher to read for their comments. Remember, you do not have to take everyone's comments on board, if you disagree with something then trust your own judgment. Your writing style will say as much to the admissions tutor as the content. After all, for every course at Oxford or Cambridge you will have to express your ideas very well in weekly essays.

We are now going to read part of another applicant's Personal Statement that details her work experience. Helena applied to read Medicine at Cambridge and was invited for interview:

■ Excerpt from Helena's Personal Statement

I organised some work experience in the orthopaedic wing of Nottingham Hospital and at my local GP clinic. At Nottingham Hospital, I shadowed the doctors on their ward round, watched a number of knee replacements and observed fracture clinic which made me realise how such a simple procedure can dramatically increase the quality of life in older people. This is such a stark contrast with my experiences in Uganda where living to 70 is seen as something of a miracle. A further thing I learnt from my work experience is the importance of patient–doctor relationships, and this is one of the factors which really draws me to Medicine. I saw this most particularly in my work experience with a GP where I saw him take on a central role of trust within the community.

I have had much opportunity to develop my interpersonal skills. During my Sixth Form I worked with underprivileged children at an after-school club in London. I have volunteered in a charity shop and this year I am volunteering one day a week at St Peter's Hospice in Green Town. I am able to easily relate to people and enjoy meeting, getting to know and trying to help different people. I used this skill when I was deputy head girl of my school, where I was involved in talking to students and helping them with any problems they might have. I keep up to date with the news, reading about medical developments in the *BMJ* and the *New Scientist*.

Your comments:

My comments:

Helena has clearly gone to a great deal of trouble to organise work experience. She has weaved her experiences into her narrative about why she wants to do Medicine and why she thinks she would be good at it.

Finally, we are going to read another Personal Statement in its entirety. Imogen applied to Oxford to read French and Italian. She was invited to interview:

■ Imogen's Personal Statement

In a world where increasing numbers of people speak English, it may seem superfluous for students to put their efforts into acquiring foreign languages. For me, however, language is not just a means by which we communicate, but the barrier of language often hides whole worlds of literature and culture which can remain inaccessible, even through translation. For this reason, language as a whole is a source of fascination for me, resulting in a desire to focus on Italian, which I did at A level, and French, a language I very much enjoyed at GCSE and which I feel complements Italian well. I have therefore resolved to take a one year French A-level course during my gap year, enabling me to study it at university.

I think literature portrays language at its best, as it is the means by which a language displays the full range of its versatility and the essence of the people who communicate through it. It often offers a window into the culture it describes, which I feel is especially well achieved by Natalia Ginzburg. After studying *Le Voci della Sera* at A level, I read *La Strada che Va in Citta* and *E Stato Cosi*, finding that her depiction of the various female characters strongly impresses upon the reader the difficulties faced by these women in the light of their religion and community. One sympathises easily with them as they struggle to find happiness, owing largely to Ginzburg's simple and often stark narrative. Similarly, I admire Primo Levi for the style in which he narrates, maintaining a dignified approach to the experiences he describes. In *Se Non Ora, Quando?* his depiction of Italy is striking: an *oasis* of freedom, where Jews and Christians are indistinguishable.

57

To help improve my French I have read various works of literature and philosophy. Interested in the problem of evil through Philosophy A level, I read Voltaire's *Zadig*, which demonstrates how suffering is unavoidable, but that sense and perseverance will see a man through. This, however, does little to solve the theological problem of evil. Nor does *Candide* twelve years later, but it highlights flaws in the ideology that *tout est au mieux*, or 'all is for the best', and points forward to suggest how to live happily in spite of evil. I subscribe to the literary magazine *Virgule*, through which I discovered Pierre de Ronsard, in whom I was delighted to find traces of Petrarch, by whom I have read some *Canzoniere*, and numerous classical authors that I have studied. I read a selection of *Les Amours*, and found that there was much opportunity for intertextual comparison with the texts I have studied in the past.

Last summer I worked as an au pair in France, which improved my French enormously, not only giving me an understanding of French daily life, but also valuable experience of the world of work. At school I was awarded the Prize for Classics and Italian, for linguistic success and contribution to these areas. Outside academic concerns, I was a Managing Director of a Young Enterprise company in Year 12, and have completed the Silver Duke of Edinburgh award, as well as a qualification in youth leadership, which I hope have made me responsible and motivated. In addition to playing the piano, I sang in two choirs at school and continue to take lessons, focusing on Italian arias. Alongside my studies this year, I follow Italian current affairs by transcribing the TG2 news, and am taking conversation classes weekly. I am also taking classes at the Institut Français in London to help me become more fluent in French, and shall continue to read avidly, exploring as many authors as possible.

Your comments:

My comments:

Imogen comes across as a diligent and highly interested student. She is widely read and seems to be an interesting person. Would you interview her?

■ The extra Personal Statement on the Oxford form

As well as writing a Personal Statement, you can choose to write an extra Personal Statement on the Oxford application form. You do not have to write anything in this section of the form but it seems a good opportunity to write something interesting. Note that the admissions tutors will have both forms so do not duplicate anything from your UCAS form. Just like the UCAS form, there is no word limit but a (very small) space limit. The idea behind the extra Personal Statement in the Oxford form is for you to say something specific about why you are suited to the Oxford course, as the UCAS form goes to all the universities that you apply to. There is no longer a separate application form for Cambridge and it is not yet clear if there is room for extra information like this in the Supplementary Application Questionnaire. Here are some examples:

■ Adam's extra Personal Statement

(Remember Adam applied to read Economics at Cambridge. N.B. At the time of going to press, I believe that there is no longer space on the Supplementary Application Questionnaire (Cambridge) to write an extra Personal Statement (although it used to be the case that there was). However, Oxford is retaining this space. Since application procedures can vary each year I have retained the example below for the extra Personal Statement for Cambridge. In any case, it is useful for Oxford applicants to see the examples.)

I am particularly interested in studying Economics at Cambridge as the faculty stresses its commitment to public policy, and I share the view of its importance to the functioning of our daily lives. The course is particularly suited to my interests as I would have the opportunity to specialise in some areas, such as Development Economics and I would enjoy the academic rigour of applying maths to the analysis of Economics. Furthermore, I would be able to draw from my other interests such as politics and history to augment my study of Economics. I have started to use SPSS software in order to enhance my theoretical backbone of econometrics and because I enjoy using quantitative methods.

I find the collegiate nature of the university attractive because I cannot get enough of talking about the subject, and nothing is as enjoyable as to share one's interest with others who feel the same way about it! Also, as someone who values perspective, I think that discussing issues with people from different disciplines would facilitate the exchange of ideas and present new angles from which to address points of interest. I am also excited at the opportunity to discuss ideas in supervisions with people who are at the forefront of their field and who are engaged in active research.

> **Your comments:**

My comments:

Adam has researched how the Faculty of Economics defines itself and what its values are and has commented about how this would suit him. He has said something in this section that he would not have been able to say on his UCAS Personal Statement as it is Cambridge specific. If you have not got anything Oxford or Cambridge specific to say then it is best not to write anything.

Imogen wrote an extra Personal Statement for the Oxford form:

Having been uncertain at the age of 16 which subjects to continue, I am now looking forward with confidence and enthusiasm to the challenge of completing French A level in the coming year before embarking on a Modern Languages degree course. The emphasis that the Modern Languages course at Oxford places upon literature mirrors my own enthusiasm for French and Italian literature, and I was particularly thrilled to note that several lecturers have expertise in the works of Primo Levi, for whom I have great admiration and would love to study at a higher level. As I am thinking of becoming a teacher, the idea of the year abroad greatly appeals, as it would give me valuable experience of teaching, whilst improving my linguistic fluency to a high level.

> **Your comments:**

My comments:

Imogen has explained why she is particularly interested in the Oxford Course. She has also used the space to explain in further depth her unusual A-level choices (she did not take French at A level but wanted to study it at university).

We have seen that the extra Personal Statement can be used to explain why you are particularly suited to the course or to explain a personal circumstance. However, this is not the time to explain how your grandmother's illness may have affected your exam results. If you genuinely believe that there is a personal circumstance (such as illness) that will have affected your exam results but that if it had not been for that then you would have achieved better grades then you can fill out a special form called the Cambridge Access Scheme. This is also open to students who come from a school that is not used to sending students to Oxford or Cambridge. By filling out this extra form you are guaranteed an interview. There is no equivalent form at Oxford although your teacher can write a separate letter explaining your circumstances.

■ Checklist

Have you understood?

☐   You are going to have to start working on your Personal Statement many months before the application is due in.

Follow it up

☐   Have you written the first draft of your Personal Statement?

07 Extra exams

For some subjects, you may have to take an exam when you get to Oxford or Cambridge, before your interview or for some subjects you may have to take an exam well before the interview in your own school. See below for a list. Oxford has a very standardised approach whereas Cambridge has a more ad hoc policy to exams that varies from college to college.

Straight from the horse's mouth

Tests such as BMAT, LNAT and HAT are crucial in deciding who is interviewed as are the new maths and physics tests and the new tests coming in English and PPE.

Admissions Tutor, Oxford

The process is different at Oxford and Cambridge although there are some similarities. The bottom line is that tutors want to choose students who will get the best grades in their final year. But how do you know who these students are? All the students applying have or are predicted to get all As at A level. Also A level often tests factual recall but what other skills are needed at university?

The answer is that being able to read a passage and understand what can and can't be surmised by that passage is one of the things that is important – in other words – critical analysis. Not only is this a useful skill at university when conducting research for your essays but also it is important in life in general. In fact, the top employers, for example, for civil service fast stream and investment banks, have been testing these skills for years in very similar tests.

Applying to Oxford

The first thing you have to do is go to the prospectus or the Oxford admissions website to find out if your subject requires tests. If your subject does require a test then go to the website and download the sample tests www.admissions.ox.ac.uk/interviews/tests. The test you sit will be the same at every college. It may or may not be referred to in your interview.

Applying to Cambridge

At Cambridge, for most subjects there is not a centralised system. Different colleges set different written exams at interview for the same course and different colleges may or may not set exams even for the same subject. The way to look it up is to go to www.cam.ac.uk/admissions/undergraduate/courses. You need to click on your course. On the right hand side of the next screen is a box entitled 'At a glance'. The fourth hyperlink down says 'admissions test' click on the link. A new page will come up with a list of all the colleges and the requirements for your subject. If we take the engineering page as an example: www.cam.ac.uk/admissions/undergraduate/courses/engineering/tests.html we can see that at some colleges they use the TSA, at others they use an interview only, at some they use their own test at interview and at others they use both their own test at interview and the TSA.

Apart from the subjects that require you to sit tests at interview, there are others that require you to sit a test well before your interview. These subjects and names of test are as follows:

Exam	Oxford	Cambridge
LNAT (Law)	√	√
BMAT (Medicine and Veterinary Medicine)	√	√
PPEAT (PPE)	√	
ELAT (English)	√	
HAT (History)	√	
TSA (Thinking Skills Assessment) (Computer Science Engineering Economics, Engineering, English, Land Economy, Natural Sciences and any others as the colleges see fit)		√
Maths	√	√ (STEP)
Physics and Maths for Physics	√	

BMAT and the Maths and Physics tests require specialist knowledge and facts need to be revised.

■ BioMedical Admissions Test (BMAT) for Medicine (Oxford and Cambridge) and Veterinary Science (Cambridge)

Let us start with BMAT. Some universities, including Oxford and Cambridge, require students applying for medical school and for veterinary science to sit the BMAT exam. What the medical schools then do with the scores varies. Oxford looks only at your GCSE grades and BMAT scores in order to assess whether you are to be invited to interview for medicine. Cambridge looks at all the information available to them (BMAT and

UCAS form) to see if they will invite you to interview. Either way, what is clear is that the BMAT is very important in deciding whether or not you will be accepted at Oxford and Cambridge.

Let us look more closely at BMAT and what it entails. You need to apply online to register for BMAT. BMAT stands for the BioMedical Admission Test. It is a two-hour paper that is sat at your school. There are three sections: aptitude and skills (60 minutes, multiple choice), scientific knowledge and applications (30 minutes, multiple choice) and an essay (you need to choose one title out of three) (30 minutes). There is a fee to pay for BMAT to be announced in March, which can be waived if you are in receipt of full EMA (Education Maintenance Allowance). Go to www.bmat.org.uk/faqstudent.html#gen15 for more information. In 2007 it cost £27.30. Use a pencil for the multiple choice sections and a biro for the essay question. Answer all questions, you are not penalised for wrong answers. You will have to find out the date by which you must register for BMAT but it is likely to be by the end of September or by mid-October if you pay a late entry penalty. The BMAT exam will take place on one day at the end of October or at the beginning of November.

What do you need to revise for BMAT?

BMAT requires GCSE-level knowledge of Maths and GCSE Dual Science Award knowledge of Biology, Chemistry and Physics. This does not mean hazily remembering your GCSE days. This means active revision. For many Medics, Physics and Maths may be a thing of the past – but you have to revise them thoroughly for the exam. The exam is structured such that Biology, Chemistry and Physics are equally weighted and Maths is slightly less. Go through your old exam questions, or buy a GCSE revision guide. If you have not written an essay for two years it is worth practicing and perhaps showing your old English or History teacher. Here are two essay titles that are similar to the 2007 BMAT essay questions:

- Is longevity shaking the foundations of society and changing attitudes to life and death?
- The technology of Medicine will outrun society. Discuss.

How Oxford and Cambridge use the BMAT score

Oxford and Cambridge will look at the scores of each section individually. Cambridge tutors believe that Sections 1 and 2 correlate best with Tripos performance and therefore put an emphasis on doing well in those sections. Although the first section cannot be revised for, the second section can be heavily revised for. Unfortunately for those people who write well, even if you get a very high mark for the essay, the most important thing Cambridge cares about is Sections 1 and 2. Oxford will deselect medical applicants on the basis of their GCSEs and BMAT score. This means that if these grades are low, you will not be invited to interview.

■ English Literature Aptitude Test (ELAT) for applications for English at Oxford only

The ELAT tests applicants' ability in the close reading of an unfamiliar text and the construction of a focused essay. Like the BMAT, the ELAT takes place at your school. You need to find out the date by which you need to apply. The exam takes place in late October or early November. It lasts for 90 minutes and is free of charge. The ELAT tests your skills in close reading and you will have to analyse two or three passages out of a possible six and write a comparative essay. You will have to explain why you have selected the passages that you have and indicate what you will explore through comparative analysis. There are no key texts you need to read. You will not get any marks for making reference to other writings. It is very important to look at the sample paper and go through the mark scheme. For more information go to www.elat.org. uk.The top 40% will be interviewed.

■ History Aptitude Test (HAT) for applications to History at Oxford only

The HAT is testing that you can read critically and write with clarity. You need to revise your history A-level syllabus thoroughly as you will be asked to give an example of a situation from the history periods you have studied. The best way to practise HAT is to download all the past papers and mark schemes from: www.history.ox.ac.uk/prosundergrad/applying/hat_introduction.htm.

Read one of the sample answers and mark it as if you were the admissions tutor – what do you think are the key points? Then compare your marks with the mark scheme and check that you understand what is being tested. A brief overview will show you that being able to summarise an argument without simply quoting huge chunks is considered to be very important and another point that comes through is how important it is to be focussed on your answer.

The HAT is taken at your school and is free. It lasts for two hours and will be sat on a day at the end of October or beginning of November. For an explanation of the structure of the test see www.history. ox.ac.uk/prosundergrad/applying/hat_specification.htm. The test is meant to be of a difficulty similar to the Advanced Extension Award. The interviewers will look at your score as well as your reference and qualifications to reach a decision about whom to interview. In addition a homework will need to be submitted (check the faculty website for the submission deadline) and may be used as a basis for discussion at interview. The HAT will not be discussed at interview. Oxford automatically will send the HAT to your school. In general, the people who score in the bottom 20% of HAT will be deselected.

Law National Admissions Test (LNAT) for applications to Law (Oxford and Cambridge)

If you are applying for Law at Oxford or Cambridge and indeed at a handful of other universities you will need to sit LNAT.

LNAT is a two-hour test. There are two parts, a multiple choice test for which there are 80 minutes allocated and an essay question for which there are 40 minutes allocated and you should write about 600 words. You have to go to a special centre to sit it and it is sat at a computer. No specialist knowledge is required. There is a fee to pay (£40) which will be waived if you cannot afford it (see www.lnat.ac.uk/2007/help/money.html). The multiple choice test is about reading a passage and answering some questions about it. Answer all questions, you are not penalised for wrong answers.

It is very important to familiarise yourself with the test. Go to the LNAT website and practice the questions on www.lnat.ac.uk/2007/preparation/practice.html. The LNAT can be taken from early September at centres across the country. If you cannot afford the fee, students can be reimbursed. Go to www.lnat.ac.uk/2007/help/money.html.

You will have to identify main arguments, assumptions in multiple choice questions and the ways in which arguments link together. The essay can be no longer than four A4 typed pages. A good way to practise the essay is to get involved in debating in your school. If your school does not currently have a debating club why not set one up? Your English teacher or Head of Sixth Form may be able to help you. It will enable you to think on your feet. It is very helpful to read the commentary on the sample test found at www.lnat.ac.uk/2007/documents/sampletest05solutions.pdf and note the hints, tips and insights that they provide.

Maths Entrance Test (MET) (Oxford)

If you are applying for Mathematics or Maths with Computer Science, Philosophy, Statistics or Computer Science you will need to take this test. It will be sat at your school on one day at the end of October or beginning of November. Your school will be sent the papers automatically. The test lasts two and a half hours. The Maths exams are based on C1 and C2 of A-level Maths and not on Further Maths at all. It is very important to check you have covered the syllabus. However, you are advised to take as much Maths as is offered to you, including STEP or AEA. Go to www.maths.ox.ac.uk/files/imported/prospective-students/undergraduate/specimen-tests/syllabus.pdf to see the actual syllabus for the exam. Calculators are not permitted.

■ Physics and Maths for Physics (Oxford)

This is a two-hour test. Calculators are not permitted. You need to revise all the physics and maths that you have learnt at school. Shortlisting is largely based on the results of the aptitude tests. It is very important to look at the syllabus: www.physics.ox.ac.uk/admissions/syllabus.htm. The Physics course at Oxford is highly mathematical and it is important that you demonstrate strong mathematical ability.

■ Philosophy, Politics and Economics Aptitude Test for applications (PPEAT) to PPE at Oxford only

This consists of two parts: a multiple choice test and an essay. The essay lasts for 30 minutes. The PPEAT will take place at your school and is free. Go to www.tsa.cambridgeassessment.org.uk/ppe for more information. It lasts two hours and will be sat on a day in late October or early November. As well as revising critical analysis, it is also a good idea to revise some basic maths.

■ The Thinking Skills Assessment (TSA) for a variety of subjects at Cambridge only

Colleges can use the TSA for any subject although they are currently being used for Computer Science, Economics, Engineering, Land Economy and Natural Sciences. This test can be taken online or as a pen-and-paper test and is taken when you go to interview at Cambridge. There are critical thinking questions and questions that require problem-solving skills in multiple choice format. The test lasts 90 minutes. The following document is particularly useful in under-standing what is being asked of you: http://tsa.ucles.org.uk/pdf/tsa_description.pdf and make sure you do the specimen test http://tsa.ucles.org.uk/pdf/demo_test.pdf. The different types of question under the problem-solving category: one that involves sifting through information to identify what is important, finding a situation that has a similar structure to another. It is important to have an awareness of the maths you need for the test which can be found on page 7 of the following document: http://tsa.ucles.org.uk/pdf/tsa_description.pdf.

There are various kinds of critical thinking questions which include summarising the main point, identifying an assumption, drawing a conclusion, considering what weakens an argument, identifying flaws in an argument, understanding the structure of an argument and applying principles. Each question is worth one mark but some questions are harder than others. Make sure you move onto the next question if you are stuck.

■ Sixth Term Examination Papers (STEP) (Oxford and Cambridge) (Maths)

Cambridge almost always asks for a STEP paper in Maths as part of a conditional offer for Maths (and Maths with Physics) and it can also be used as part of a conditional offer for Engineering, Computer Science, Natural Sciences and Oxford sometimes does. No further mathematical knowledge over and above the core Maths A level syllabus is needed for STEP. The exam is taken in June at the same time as your A level.

Straight from the horse's mouth

The questions [for STEP] are of a searching kind designed to test qualities like insight originality, grasp of broader issues and the ability to use standard techniques in unusual ways and situations.

Cambridge Prospectus, 2008

You sit STEP at your school or at a recognised centre after your A levels. Speak to our examinations officer as soon as you can. If your school cannot help prepare you for STEP, Cambridge runs an intensive study school. Speak to the admissions tutor for more details.

■ Advanced Extension Awards (AEA) (Cambridge only) (many subjects)

Like STEP, AEA requires no additional subject knowledge to your A-level syllabus and assesses your ability in critical thinking and logic. It can be taken in many subjects and is taken after your A levels. Some colleges make offers involving AEA as an alternative to a standard offer. These are Christ's, Peterhouse and Emmanuel. Even if you are applying to a college that does not make offers involving AEAs it is a good idea to take them if they are on offer at your school and write that you intend to take them on your personal statement as they are looked upon favourably as they are known to really stretch you.

■ Preparation for logic-based tests

To help with preparation for the TSA and LNAT, and the first section of the BMAT, as well as logic problems in the Maths exams, it would be wise to look at critical thinking materials. Look at the past papers and mark schemes for the critical thinking A levels and AEA that the exam boards AQA and OCR set. Go to: www.aqa.org.uk/qual/gce/critical_thinking_new.php; www.ocr.org.uk/Data/publications/key_documents/AS_A_Level8695.pdf; www.ocr.org.uk/qualifications/asa_levelgceforfirstteachingin2008/critical_thinking/index.html and www.ocr.org.uk/qualifications/aea/critical_thinking/index.html.

■ Tests for subjects other than the ones covered

If you are applying for any other subjects you will probably have to do an exam directly before your interview. For past papers go to: www.admissions.ox.ac.uk/interviews/tests. However, this list is subject to change. You must consult the relevant websites regularly to check. If you are in doubt, give the admissions tutor a ring to clarify. Cambridge colleges set their own individual exam. Have a look on the individual colleges' websites for guidance about the exams and/or contact the admissions tutor to ask for sample material. It may be that in addition or as an alternative to an exam, you are given an article to read and discuss in your interview. Be prepared for this and take a highlighter and pen.

Even if you do well in this test (you will probably be told your mark in your interview and your answers may also be discussed) you cannot rest on your laurels. You need to show extra sparkle in the interview as well as having a good mark in the written test. This is the subject of the next chapter.

■ Checklist

Have you understood?

☐   In some subjects you have to take a test well before your interview, often in your own school.

☐   The best preparation is to go through all the past papers.

Follow it up

☐   What is the date of your exam?

☐   Have you downloaded all the past papers?

☐ The key is to make sure that you are able to read a text, understand it and explain it to someone else, noting the main points of the argument and any assumptions or flaws. You could try taking some newspaper editorials from a good newspaper and explain it as above to somebody else.

Further reading

Critical thinking and problem solving

Mike Bryon, *The Ultimate Psychometric Test Book*, Kogan Page Ltd, London, 2006.
A. Fisher, *Critical Thinking: An Introduction*, Cambridge University Press, Cambridge, 2001.
Andrea Shavick, *Management Level Psychometric and Assessment Tests*, How to Books Ltd, Oxford, 2005.
Willfred Hodges, *Logic*, Penguin Books Ltd, London (2nd Revised Edition), 2001.
Robert Martin, *There are Two Errors in the the Title of This Book*, Broadview Press, Canada (1st Edition), 1992.
Peter Rhodes, *Practice Tests for Critical Verbal Reasoning (Succeed at Psychometric Testing)*, Hodder Arnold, London, 2006.
Mark Sainsbury, *Logical Forms*, Wiley Blackwell, Iowa, USA,1991.

BMAT

Taylor, Hutton and Hutton's *Passing the UK Clinical Aptitude Test (UKCAT) and BMAT*, Law Matters Publishing (2nd Revised Edition), 2007.

Websites

For similar types of questions to the critical thinking components of BMAT, ELAT, HAT, LNAT, PPEAT, TSA (although these ones are used for graduate recruitment) go to:

■ www.shl.com/shl/en-int/candidatehelpline
■ www.shldirect.com/example_questions.html

08 Going to your interview

Many universities do not interview candidates at all. They judge you entirely on your predicted grades, reference and Personal Statement. However, Oxford and Cambridge will never offer you a place without an interview. (Even if you are unfortunate enough to be too ill to attend in person, you will have to do a telephone interview often interacting with resources on the internet.) Let's spend a moment reflecting on why Oxford and Cambridge have this policy and what it means for you.

As well as attending lectures, you will also attend tutorials (these are called 'supervisions' in Cambridge but they are the same thing) which are often 'one-to-one' with your tutor. These tutorials are an hour a week with the same tutor. In these tutorials you will present your essay you have written from extensive research in the week and your tutor will critically analyse and discuss various points with you. In order for these tutorials to be successful you will have to 'get on' with your tutor and you both should be intellectually stimulated from the tutorial. The tutor or tutors interviewing you are most likely to be the ones giving you the tutorials so they are directly assessing whether they can work with you and whether they will enjoy it.

Your comments:

Imagine you are the tutor. What sort of qualities would you look for in a student?

My comments:

I would want evidence that the student has an inquiring mind, is pleasant and polite, seriously interested in the subject, flexible enough to be able to engage with new ideas, possibly fun.

Straight from the horse's mouth

Candidates should be intellectually robust, inquisitive and ambitious.

Admissions Tutor, Cambridge

It should be clear that in order to see if a candidate has these qualities an interview is entirely necessary and these attributes cannot be assessed by the UCAS/Oxford/Cambridge form alone.

Straight from the horse's mouth

What can you expect in an interview?

- *Structured but informal discussion*
- *Challenging and open-ended question*
- *Questions on school work outside of your comfort zone*
- *Problem solving/critical thinking.*

Admissions Tutor, Cambridge

Your comments:

Assuming you do have these qualities (as otherwise you would not be applying) how are you going to display them?

My comments:

The key here is, when answering their questions, to think aloud as much as possible. If you need a bit more time to think or you did not quite get your head around the question, simply say, 'I'm sorry, would you mind repeating the question' or 'Am I right in thinking that what you are getting at is . . .? Do not be afraid to ask for clarification. It shows a willingness to engage with the question and the quest for clarity is itself a good thing and it demonstrates that you are precise and accurate.

Thinking aloud means going through the thought process out loud. It is a bit like when you are asked to show all your workings in a maths calculation instead of just writing down the answer. The advantage to thinking aloud is that if you go wrong somewhere the interviewer might say, 'are you sure about that?' If necessary you can always ask for a piece of paper to do a calculation: this is probably very useful in physics for jotting down an equation or biology for drawing a diagram of a cell. Asking for things such as a piece of paper shows confidence in yourself. It shows that you are in control of your ideas and are able to interact with the tutors, regardless of their academic status, which is important as you will have to interact with them regularly if you get in.

Straight from the horse's mouth

My last interview was the most challenging of the four interviews I had, simply because of the way in which I was interviewed. There were two professors, who bombarded me with a series of questions in quick succession, constantly interrupting my answers to ask why I had said that, where I was getting my evidence from and could I give more examples of the point I was making.

Oxford Applicant

If you are applying for a humanities subject, like PPE (Politics, Philosophy and Economics), to show you are thinking aloud you could say: 'Well, I would go about this question by breaking the problem down into stages, first I would consider . . .'. As well as showing that you are thinking logically and considering the problem without giving a knee-jerk answer, it also buys you some more time for your brain to tick things over. Don't be afraid to give an answer even if you think it is wrong (of course it is better to give one that is right!). Giving no answer at all shows you are not able to think on your feet or be innovative. Giving an answer, in stages, allows the interviewer to prompt you at the stage where you may be going wrong, giving you the maximum chance of giving an answer in the right ball park. In most subjects, there is no right or wrong answer anyway, and it is the logic you employ that is of interest to the interviewers.

Straight from the horse's mouth

The interview is trying to recreate a supervision. If you handle a question badly acknowledge it and move on. What you say is more important than how you say it.

Admissions Tutor, Cambridge

Read the following account of Adam's Economics interviews at Cambridge and analyse how the tutors are trying to see how you think. Adam had two interviews, one subject specific interview and one general interview.

■ Adam's experience of the Cambridge interviews

Two weeks before my interview I was sent an interview pack from Cambridge which contained an article that I had read in advance of the interview, a few maps of the college and of Cambridge, some information about the interviews and a food voucher for the food hall.

My interview was at midday. I could have stayed over the night before but I live close so I did not. There were no designated student helpers and I got a bit lost in the college (it is very large) so I asked some people for help and directions. I would recommend going to the Porter's Lodge if you get very lost and they will direct you.

My first interview was the specialist interview for Economics. I was interviewed by two female economists, who invited me to sit down on a couch as I entered the room where the interview took place. One interviewer sat directly in front of me and the other sat at a desk looking to the side. The interviewer who sat in front of me was the main interviewer, as the other interviewer hardly ever intervened and just took notes diligently. The interview started with the principal interviewer asking me about what current events in the news had interested me most. I responded by talking about Northern Rock. She asked me why I was interested with what was happening at the time with Northern Rock. I told her that it stemmed from my great interest in Economics and related it to out-of-class reading I had done on the subject of not only Economics but on banking systems. The interview continued in that same tone and style. It was a very sober, tense environment. The interview was very formal and no time was lost to discussions that did not relate to Economics.

I was sent an article a couple of weeks prior to the interview. And I was asked a few questions on it. The answers basically related back to my A-level knowledge of the subject. Then I was given a paragraph on Economics and was told to comment on it. The comment could be about anything I wanted to say or thought about the paragraph. It had some errors, not grammatical, but rested on dubious theory such as 'if you raise taxes, people will spend more' whereas I have been taught that if you raise taxes people will spend less.

Then they asked me a mathematical problem. They gave me a whiteboard to solve it on. It was a geometric problem. The problem was that there were two pieces of carpet and you had to cover an entire room with those two pieces of carpet. The trick was you could only do one cut. This seemed to me to be impossible. I was told to do what I could and I talked through the logic of finding the solution to that problem. I was stopped after around 30 seconds. After the maths question, the interviewers asked me if I had any questions. I asked them about fiscal policy and we engaged in a small discussion and then the interview came to an end.

My general interview was very relaxed. The admissions tutor asked me very general questions such as 'Why Cambridge?', 'Why this college?'. I was asked questions such as 'Tell me five words your friends would use to describe you'. I was also told to describe an object as if I was on the telephone with the admissions tutor and they could not see the object. After I described the object he asked me why I thought he asked me that. The off-beat, laid back style characterised the interview. It was a very pleasant experience. The interviewer's questions were either very general and expected or very diverse, unusual and startling.

Your comments:

What answer would you have given to 'why do you think I asked you to describe an object as if I couldn't see it?'

My comments:

I think the tutor was trying to see how articulate Adam was and also if he could look beyond the question and analyse why it had been asked. Very often the question itself is not as interesting as the reason why it has been asked.

Read the two detailed accounts of interviews for languages at Oxford and Cambridge below. What are the discernible differences between the interviews at Oxford and at Cambridge?

■ Imogen's experience of the Oxford interviews

Imogen applied for French and Italian (Modern Languages) at Oxford

I was called approximately ten days before my provisional date, but the letter did nothing except confirm that I had been called. There were no times or details given. Upon arrival at Oxford, the night before the interviews began, I learnt that the next day I had a language test and an Italian interview, and a French interview the following day.

Oxford prefers not to allow candidates to make their own way to interviews, in case they get lost, so each college has a general waiting room and a group of current undergraduate helpers to accompany everyone. On the morning of the test, all the modern linguists gathered in the waiting room, and we were shown to classrooms where we had to take a grammar test in each of the languages we were applying for, except those we were intending to study *ab initio* (from scratch). I therefore sat tests in French and Italian, lasting an hour in total, and consisting of translation and multiple choice.

My Italian interview took place at Balliol (I applied to St Anne's), because there is no Italian fellow at St Anne's. A student helper took me to Balliol, and I was given an Italian poem to look at. This was discussed in my interview, which was conducted by only one interviewer, and I was then asked to recount my Personal Statement, because he hadn't seen it. We then discussed various books I have read and surprisingly, did not speak any Italian.

The next morning I had a French interview at St Anne's, which was conducted by three interviewers. Again I was given a passage to read, again in English, which was discussed with one of the interviewers. There was a conversation in French with a second interviewer, which covered some literature and my reasons for studying French. Last, the third interviewer asked some slightly more in depth questions about the importance of literature, and the relationship between literature and philosophy (I had made some references to philosophy in my Personal Statement).

I had been told that I would be allowed to leave Oxford at 10 a.m. the following morning, but that some candidates would be required to stay until later the next day to attend interviews at other colleges, to which they had been pooled. This is because the Oxford pooling system is different to that of Cambridge, in that it takes place before any firm offers or rejections are made. It is also possible to have an interview at a college to which you have been pooled, and then still be made an offer by the original college to which you applied. I was not one of these 'pooled' candidates. Indeed, none of the candidates at my particular college were pooled, and we were all allowed to go home.

Inside the actual interview

Italian 1 (one interviewer)
This was a very strange interview. I was given an Italian poem (*Canzonetta sulle sirene catodiche by Magrelli*) to read and make notes on before I was called in.

- I had to describe aspects of the poem which I found interesting.
- I was then asked to summarise my Personal Statement as he hadn't seen it before.
- Then he asked me why I thought that Primo Levi was a good writer, told me that his book was originally rejected by Natalia Ginzburg and asked what I felt about that.

- The conversation then moved on to Dante, and he wanted to know how I had approached my study of *L'Inferno*, and which of the canti I had enjoyed.
- I was then given the opportunity to ask him a question.

There was no Italian conversation.

Italian 2 (two interviewers)
I was given a poem in English.

- Again, the poem was discussed in depth, but this time I was pushed to interpret bits which were harder to understand, rather than just comment on bits I liked.
- The interviewer then picked up on the Primo Levi in my Personal Statement, and asked me what I thought of the quote 'After Auschwitz, no more poetry' with reference to the philosophy I studied at school.
- There was a brief conversation in Italian, focusing on current affairs and places I had visited in Italy.
- Again I was allowed to ask a question.

French 1 (three interviewers)
The passage was in English, it was an extract from the works of Edgar Allen Poe.

- I was asked questions about the tone of the passage, what situation I thought the extract was taken from and how I felt the episode would conclude.
- French conversation – why I wanted to study French as opposed to any other language, what I felt the themes were in the film *Jules et Jim* by Francois Truffaut (the essay I sent up was based on this film) and what I felt the film said about the difference between the French and the Germans during the war.
- I was asked a series of questions, including: why is it important to study literature? What is the difference between literature and philosophy? What French book have I recently read that I enjoyed? I talked about *La Princesse de Cleves*.

French 2 (two interviewers)
The poem was in French. There was a note at the top saying that I should try to understand the poem, but not worry if I didn't know all the vocabulary, because I would be asked which bits of the poem I found most interesting and was not expected to understand it all.

- However, I was then fired a series of questions on every verse of the poem, and interrupted during every answer to be further questioned on why I thought that, where I was getting my information from, and could I give more examples to back up my point. Luckily, I had been placed in a library to read through the passage, and so had looked up all the unfamiliar vocabulary. Moral of the story – don't believe the kindly-worded instructions!

- One of the interviewers then said he was intrigued as to my interest in Ronsard, and we discussed where the major Petrarchian influences were in the poetry.
- Then followed French conversation where I had to talk about my work placement in Le Touquet, and what I thought the differences were between French and British holidaymakers.
- Then I was allowed to ask a question.

Madeleine's experience of the Cambridge interviews

Madeleine applied for Modern and Medieval Languages at Cambridge

Shortly after I had sent off my UCAS form, Cambridge contacted me by letter to give me details of the written work they required, which in my case was two essays; one for Latin and one for Italian. I therefore wrote a discursive essay in English for the Latin requirement, and a short essay based on an A-level topic in Italian. These essays were due early in November.

I was then called to interview, again by letter, which arrived roughly halfway through November, and was told all the details and times of the tests and interviews I would be expected to sit, which all took place on one day in the first half of December.

I stayed in college the night before my interviews, due to an early start the next day, which I would highly recommend as it gives one the opportunity to get used to the surroundings, talk to current students and it means that it isn't a great rush in the morning before interview. I had to sit a test first, and as a language applicant I had to choose one of my languages in which to answer. In my case, it had to be Italian, but as it turned out, very little of the test was actually in the foreign language. There was a passage to be read, in English, which I had to summarise in a foreign language (Italian), and then answer a very broad essay question in English. The test lasted an hour.

My first interview was a couple of hours later, so I took the opportunity to have lunch with some friends who were also applying to other colleges, whilst making sure I left myself plenty of time to get to the interview, which was for the Latin side of my application. I was given some Latin poetry to read, try to understand and analyse, and this was then discussed in the interview. I was also questioned about the essay I had sent up, and was given some general questions about why I had applied for the course and what my gap year plans were. In this particular interview, there were two interviewers.

Following this was my Italian interview, which was conducted by one person only. Again, I was given a passage to try to understand and talk about, and then we discussed the literature that I was studying for my

A2. Finally, she asked me a couple of questions in Italian to test my standard of speaking, focusing where I had visited in Italy.

After this, I was free to leave, with nothing else to do but wait for the result. At Cambridge the results are all given out on one day, shortly after Christmas, and this date is stated in advance. There will be one of three possible results given on this day, either an acceptance, a rejection or the news that you have been placed in the 'winter pool', which means that there is a possibility that another college will accept you based on the strength of your UCAS form. Acceptance or rejection from this pool can be held until as late as the end of January, during which time there is the possibility of being called for further interviewing.

Inside the actual interviews

Latin (two interviewers)

I was given a 20 line passage of Ovid's *Metamorphoses*, about half an hour before the start of the interview, and left in the library to look at it. I was then escorted up to the interview room.

I was addressed first by the general admissions tutor for Modern and Medieval Languages, who asked me what had brought me to my choice of languages (Latin and Italian), and which aspects of the course at Cambridge appealed. She then asked me lots of questions about the gap year I intended to take, how I thought it would be beneficial to me and how I planned to keep my study skills alive whilst I was away.

The rest of the interview was conducted by the Latin lecturer, who started by asking me some grammatical questions about the passage I had looked at. I had to translate bits of it, and then identify some literary techniques used to enhance the meaning. We then talked about the passage in general, focusing more on the themes and general storyline. He then mentioned the essay I had sent up, which was an analysis of Book I of Virgil's *Aeneid*. He questioned me quite closely on one comment I had made; so closely that the point came where I could no longer defend myself!

We discussed my Personal Statement, in particular the references I had made to Linear B, an ancient Mycenaean language, and I was asked what reading I had done to develop this unusual interest. Last, he asked me to imagine that I was talking to someone who had never studied Classics before, and to recommend them one book to read and explain my choice.

Italian (one interviewer)

There was no pre-reading for this interview, I went straight in. The interview began with some questions on my background in Italian. We then moved swiftly onto literature, in particular Pirandello's *Sei Personaggi in Cerca d'Autore*, which I had just begun at school. She asked me what I thought of it so far, and how I thought it might develop. She then produced a short text for me to look at. I read it aloud so that she could hear my accent, and she asked me to translate what I could of it. It was a very abstract opening to a novel (*Se Una Notte D'Inverno Un Viaggiatore* by Italo Calvino), and as the Pirandello play mentioned above is also quite abstract, we compared the two.

Afterwards, we talked in Italian for a bit, focusing on places I had been in Italy and current affairs (including some basics such as who the Prime Minister of Italy is etc.) This interview struck me as being very informal, that is, we did not sit across from each other, but at a small table, and she did not take any notes.

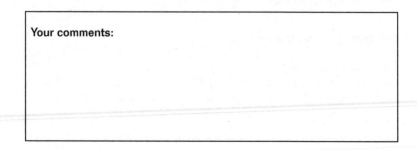

Your comments:

My comments:

Although there are some logistical differences between Oxford and Cambridge interviews, the style of the actual interviews is very similar. However, within the universities, different colleges have different interview practices and you should look at the individual college websites for further information.

■ Differences between Oxford and Cambridge in the interview process

You will have seen that the interview process differs between Oxford and Cambridge. Here is a summary of the main differences between the two universities.

- Cambridge interviews span one day only, Oxford between two and five.
- At Oxford it is possible to have interviews at other colleges through the pooling system (so bring an umbrella!), at Cambridge you will be recalled in January if necessary.
- Cambridge will tell you your interview date well in advance, Oxford will give you short notice, and expect you to know when to arrive by the 'provisional date' section in the prospectus. Oxford reserves the right to call a candidate to interview any time up until a week before the provisional date given.

- Cambridge makes known individual interview start times and locations in advance, Oxford does not.
- The Oxford pooling is done 'pre-offer', Cambridge conducts pooling afterwards.
- Oxford will inform you of their decision before Christmas, Cambridge after.

Interview tips

- Try to smile and look alert but relaxed. You are putting on the 'Me show'. You are showing how clever, but not conceited you are and how great you are to work with. They are like a TV company assessing if they want to buy your show. They are also assessing your potential. You don't have a PhD (doctorate) in your subject yet, but are you someone who could contribute to the field?
- Remember: Turn off your mobile phone – even though it can happen to the best of us, it always seems rude when a mobile phone rings.
- You may be given a text to consider directly before your interview. Make sure you have a pen and highlighter with you and actively read the text by underlining relevant phrases or words and writing notes and question marks in the margins.
- Smile and walk with purpose into the interview room.
- Have a firm handshake.
- Prepare questions you want to ask.
- Be punctual and allow plenty of time for the journey. It is useful to have a contact number in the event that you may be delayed.

What shall I wear?

The interviews take place in December, and both Oxford and Cambridge can be very cold, so make sure you wear layers – take an extra jumper or cardigan.

While we are talking about the 'Me show', let's discuss what to wear. Boys – I would wear a nice shirt and trousers. It's probably unnecessary to wear a suit. Academics are not known to be the most smartly dressed people. However, you need to look presentable, this means you need to be clean (no mud under your fingernails), shaven, make sure you hair is reasonably kempt (even if the latest style is 'bedhead'). No jewellery unless you are extremely attached to it although a watch is a good idea. Clean shoes. You want to be bright eyed so go to bed early for the whole week before your interview.

Girls – this is probably not the time to turn up in jeans and your boyfriend's jumper. Similarly it is unnecessarily formal to wear a suit. I think girls should wear black trousers and a nice shirt or top, maybe with a jacket. This is not the time to wear your sexiest-knee high boots or your lowest neckline. It is sad that women are judged on what they wear and although there is no reason why an intelligent girl should not be sexy, don't prove the point at the interview. You are dressing up as a very clever, very articulate young lady. Your hair should not be in your face as it is distracting for you and the interviewer to have to keep moving it. A simple necklace and a watch is good. No dangly earrings – again, it's distracting. If you want to wear a skirt, make sure it is at least knee length. The point is your clothes should not speak louder than you. Your clothes should complement you.

◼ Body language

Although it is natural in an interview situation, do not sit there with your arms crossed. It is a very defensive position and screams out 'no confidence'. Make an effort to sit with your arms open or on your lap. When you speak it is a good idea to gesticulate with your arms as it adds expression. However, don't overdo it. Don't bite your nails or fiddle with your hair. Often we exhibit certain mannerisms when we are thinking. It may be worth getting someone to video you when you talk to see if you have some unconscious mannerisms that are unflattering. Lean forwards, not back and sit up straight – to show interest. Speak slowly. We speak much more quickly than we realise – so slow down! Do not speak in a monotone – moderate your voice by using highs and lows. Do not fold your arms or cross your legs – these are defensive gestures that suggest you are scared to open up.

◼ Preparation

Revise all your A-level subjects, particularly the one which you are planning to study at University – if this is applicable. However, it is important to know all your A-level subjects in depth as you will look pretty silly if they ask you a bog standard A-level question and you don't know the answer. Also you need to revise for your A levels anyway. You will also look silly if you cannot remember what is in your Personal Statement. Take a copy with you to review the night before your interview.

Straight from the horse's mouth

I was asked some in depth questions about the importance of literature, and the relationship between literature and philosophy (I had made some references to philosophy in my Personal Statement).

Oxford Applicant

Your school can probably arrange for you to have a mock interview with someone whom you do not know. The interviewer should have a copy of your Personal Statement and reference. It is a good idea to have a mock interview as it allows you to gauge how much time to spend answering questions, lets you consider if you are speaking too quickly and in general it gives you a dry run as for many of you, your Oxbridge interview will be your first real interview. However it is important not to be overprepared as you will sound 'stale' in your interview.

Straight from the horse's mouth

We keep an eye out for candidates who are determined to make their prepared point. Students should not be overly or inadequately prepared for interview.

Admissions Tutor, Cambridge

Straight from the horse's mouth

Typical problems at interview:

Applicants are:

- *Too eager to agree/not keen to discuss/debate*
- *Well informed but cautious or uncritical in thinking*
- *Had difficulty when challenged to think for self*
- *Reluctant to engage with the unfamiliar*
- *Jump into answers without listening.*

Admissions Tutor, Cambridge

■ So what are the actual arrangements?

The college will give you an itinerary either when you arrive or in advance. It will detail everything. There will be a certain amount of waiting around and it is advisable to bring a book (that extra book you never got round to reading about your subject that you wrote about in your Personal Statement).

Straight from the horse's mouth

I had a short waiting time in the JCR before my first interview at 10 am. I then had a break of about two hours before my next interview. I spent that in the JCR reading newspapers.

Cambridge Applicant

■ Where do we eat?

Meals (breakfast, lunch and dinner) in college tend be served in very grandiose 'halls' meaning dining halls. Depending on the college often these are steeped in tradition – they may be lined in oak panelling and have famous alumni's portraits hung on the wall. The dining hall in Harry Potter was filmed in one of the college's halls (Christ Church, Oxford) so watch it to get an idea. The tables are probably long tables and at some colleges you will be served your entire meal and at others it will be self-service. You will be sitting with other (nervous) candidates, but relax and try to enjoy the company of your peers. It is easy to be intimidated by these halls but remember, Oxford and Cambridge are very old institutions, and it should not be surprising that their halls are so grand. It is all part of the experience.

Meals are served at set times in colleges. It may be that when you arrive you have already missed lunch or dinner. There are two options at this point. Either ask one of the student helpers where the JCR is where you may be able to buy a sandwich or go outside into town (which is literally on your doorstep) and go and get something to eat. It's easy to forget that Oxford and Cambridge are towns in their own right – they have all the high street shops that you are used to!

No one will tell you when to go to bed and no doubt the student helpers will show you where the college bar is after dinner. It might be nice to have a look but I would refrain from drinking. Don't worry about looking like a nerd, just say 'I am a bit nervous and think I should have an early night'. Remember you are going for the fresh-eyed look. Furthermore, it would create a very bad impression to smell of alcohol the next day.

■ Accommodation

Very often, for Oxford interviews (but not for Cambridge interviews) you will have to stay over in the college for a number of nights. Everything is paid for: all meals and accommodation. You simply need to take an overnight bag and your interview clothes. You may need to take a few shirts or tops as it may be that you have several interviews on different days. Many of the rooms will have en suite facilities (a shower or toilet in your room). Bring a towel. It may be that you are housed in an old-fashioned block in which case the showers are in cubicles but are in a general shower room. You may like to bring some flip-flops for this. People who have been to boarding school are used to these living arrangements but for people who have not lived away from home it may be a new experience – nothing to worry about though.

■ Checklist of things to bring

- ☐ Photocopies of your Personal Statement and essays
- ☐ Overnight bag – toothbrush, pyjamas etc.
- ☐ Towel

☐ Soap
☐ Flip-flops
☐ Interview clothes
☐ Hairdryer
☐ Umbrella
☐ Coat, hat, gloves, scarf
☐ Money for emergencies
☐ Highlighter
☐ Phone number of tutor or college
☐ Log book
☐ Current affairs diary
☐ Pen
☐ Notepad

■ Why can't Oxford tell me exactly how long I will be staying?

Your interview letter may say that you may have to stay for up to four days. The reason is that one of your interviews may be on day one and one may be on day two. Also you may have an exam to do on one day and an interview on another. At this point, we need to discuss the pooling system and this is one of the main differences between the Oxford and Cambridge entrance systems.

Each college can only accept a certain number of candidates. If the college has already found the students they want to fill their places but think that you are an excellent candidate, they put you into the 'pool' so that other colleges can pick you to interview if they have not filled their quota of places. You have a very good chance of getting in if you have been pooled so you don't need to be disappointed if this happens to you. You also may still get into your first choice of college.

Straight from the horse's mouth

- *3000 offers are made by preference colleges*
- *600–700 offers are made through the pool.*

Admissions Tutor, Cambridge

In your college in Oxford, a list will go up on the noticeboard detailing who has been pooled and where you should go and what time (see map of Oxford and Cambridge at back). If your name is on this list you will have to take yourself to the appropriate college. Get one of the student helpers to tell you where it is.

■ Flowchart of events

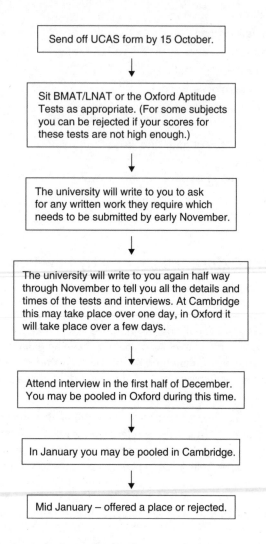

Send off UCAS form by 15 October.

↓

Sit BMAT/LNAT or the Oxford Aptitude Tests as appropriate. (For some subjects you can be rejected if your scores for these tests are not high enough.)

↓

The university will write to you to ask for any written work they require which needs to be submitted by early November.

↓

The university will write to you again half way through November to tell you all the details and times of the tests and interviews. At Cambridge this may take place over one day, in Oxford it will take place over a few days.

↓

Attend interview in the first half of December. You may be pooled in Oxford during this time.

↓

In January you may be pooled in Cambridge.

↓

Mid January – offered a place or rejected.

Straight from the horse's mouth

Relieved that my interviews were over for that day, I walked slowly back to St Anne's, but upon arrival I learnt that it is very important to check the notice board in the waiting room frequently, because there was a notice up saying that I had been asked to go for an interview at Hertford college.

Oxford Applicant

In Cambridge, pooling is slightly different. You do not attend interviews at other colleges on this trip, instead you are written to after your interviews when you return home and told to come up for an interview in January. This does mean that you will find out later than the Oxford candidates if you got in if you are put in the 'winter pool' in Cambridge.

Straight from the horse's mouth

'Around one in five applicants are pooled and of these around one in four receives an offer.'

Cambridge Admissions web pages

How to get there?

Travel information will be on the websites for Oxford and Cambridge. Also go to www.nationalexpress.com and www.nationalrail.co.uk.

I advise not to drive yourself as there is nowhere to park inside the city centres (unless you park in the Park and Ride car parks that are several miles outside the centre, requiring a bus ride to the centre). If someone is giving you a lift, you will have to say goodbye in the car as there is no parking.

Do leave plenty of time to get there. If you are really early you can wander round the shops or have a look at some of the other colleges – there is lots to do and see in Oxford and Cambridge. You could go on an open air bus tour.

Checklist

Have you understood?

- ☐ How to prepare for your interview.
- ☐ You can stay at the college for the interview period at no charge.
- ☐ The purpose of the interview is to push you to your intellectual limits and see how you cope?

Follow it up

- ☐ Have you gone through the practice questions at the back of the book for your subject?
- ☐ Have you worked out your travel arrangements?
- ☐ Have you arranged to have a mock interview at your school?
- ☐ More information about the interviews can be found in the Oxford podcasts: www.admissions.ox.ac.uk/podcasts/ and in general about interviews at: www.admissions.ox.ac.uk/interviews.
- ☐ Cambridge has produced a film on their website www.cam.uk/interviews.

09 Getting an offer and results day

■ Getting a conditional offer

Once you have had your interview, you are in the agonising position of having to wait for the result. If you applied to Oxford you will probably know before Christmas and if you applied to Cambridge then you will know by mid January. Your offer will be conditional if you have yet to complete your A levels. A conditional offer means that provided you obtain the grades that the college has stipulated, you will be given a place. This can only be confirmed on results day in August. The offer may be a general offer, for example, AAB, or specific, for example, A in Chemistry and A and B in two others. A firm or unconditional offer will be made if you already have your A-level grades, for example, if you have taken a gap year. This means you have definitely got a place.

Offers vary between colleges. Some colleges make a standard offer of AAA and others make a standard offer of AAB. Some will stipulate that you need to get 90% in certain Maths A-level modules. However in very special circumstances, such as they think you are a genius, a college can give you an EE offer (but they are also likely to ask for AEAs in this case). Christ's college, Cambridge, is known to do this. If you are made an offer which only requires you to do three A levels and you are studying for four, you may ask the admissions tutor if you can drop the fourth A level. In some cases and for arts subjects, they may agree.

If you did not get a place then do not beat yourself up and analyse what went wrong. Focus on your other universities as you may still be interviewed and you can draw on your experiences to help you.

Straight from the horse's mouth

Unsuccessful applicants almost never do anything wrong.

Admissions Tutor, Oxford

Once you have received all your offers or rejections from your universities or if you have received enough offers you inform UCAS of your firm and insurance decision. This means making a choice of where you would like to go if you get the grades, and your second choice if you don't. If you are in the unfortunate position of missing the grades for your insurance place you can still apply to university through clearing in August. For more information go to www.ucas.com. Last academic year, if you received your last decision of acceptance or rejection by 31 March then you had to come to a decision by 6 May.

If you do not get into Oxford or Cambridge remember that we are living in a globalised world and you should consider going to university in Europe or maybe one of the Ivy League universities in the USA. You will need to do a lot of preparation for this and in effect you will have a gap year. As well as applying to university, you can use your time in your gap year to do many exciting things. Ask your careers advisor for more information.

■ Making the grade

In August when the A-level exams come out, there are always mixed feelings. If you got the grades necessary to fulfil your offer then that's it – you're in. If you did not all is not lost. There are three paths to take at this point.

First, you need to get in touch with the admissions tutor as soon as possible. If you narrowly missed a grade they may let you in anyway. If something tragic happened in your family in the last few months building up to the A level then you must let the admissions tutor know, perhaps with a letter from your Head.

Straight from the horse's mouth

The colleges oversubscribe knowing that some candidates won't fulfil their offer. If you are a few marks off the admissions tutors will decide if they will still offer you a place, in a meeting that happens on results day in August.

Admissions Tutor, Cambridge

If they will not let you in then you need to ring up the admissions tutor for your subject in every college and explain your situation and see if you can get an interview. There are always students who do not get the grades and admissions tutors do want to allocate a place to an excellent student as otherwise they miss out on funding opportunities. You need to convince the tutor that you are an excellent student and you need to be able to come to an interview at short notice. If this fails, I would call up the admissions tutors at the other university (Cambridge if you originally applied for Oxford and Oxford if you originally applied for Cambridge). If you did not get good grades then you have three options. Either accept your insurance option from your original UCAS application, try to get into a different university by clearing (see UCAS website) or spend another year trying to improve your A-level grades.

If you apply again and you were unsuccessful last year, apply to a different college. If you are asked whether you applied before do not be afraid to say yes. You will not be at a disadvantage. However this is not true of Medicine – medics feel that if you are serious about studying Medicine you will accept a place elsewhere and would take a dim view of you waiting a year just because you did not get into Oxbridge.

There is a lot to be said for moving on and not obsessing about Oxford or Cambridge. We are fortunate in the UK to have many excellent universities and the people in Oxford and Cambridge are not always the best. If you are an excellent student then you will excel at anything you do and will have a happy and successful life. I have seen many students lose confidence and faith when they did not get into Oxford and Cambridge. Speak to your friends, family and teachers to discuss your feelings and get a sense of perspective. Most students feel a bit glum for a while and then look forward to attending their new university. A few students end up getting really depressed. If you feel that this is happening to you it may be worth seeking professional help – maybe from a counsellor or your GP.

Straight from the horse's mouth

More than 5000 unsuccessful applicants get three As at A level so they are not in any way unsuccessful students.

Admissions Tutor, Cambridge

Appendix 1　Glossary

Admissions tutor – The tutor especially assigned the role of selecting candidates.

Alumni – People who once went to the college but who have now graduated.

Clearing – When the A-level exam results come out in August, students who do not make their offers or, alternatively, students who get much better grades than predicted, can enter a competition for places at universities that have spare places.

Collections – Exams sat at the beginning of each term at Oxford in your college

Deferred entry – This means you would like to take a gap year (i.e. defer your entry for a year). You apply this year but will accept a place in two years' time.

Deselected – From the list of candidates who have applied for the course, some candidates will not have made it to the interview, they have been 'deselected' before the interview.

Exhibitions – A scholarship you can win in recognition of outstanding work at Oxford

Go up – Traditionally, instead of simply saying 'go to university' for Oxford and Cambridge the verb used is to 'go up' to university.

Open application – A way of applying to either Oxford or Cambridge without specifying a favoured college

Oxbridge – The collective term for Oxford and Cambridge.

Permanent Private Halls – These are like mini-colleges in Oxford, two of them (St Benet's Hall (men only) and Regent's Park College (men and women)) are for any students but the remaining five are mainly for people who are training to be in the ministry.

Pool – The pool is the place where applicants who are rejected by their first choice college are held in abeyance until another college selects them for an interview. The other college may do this for a variety of reasons, such as if they have not got enough good applicants and want to find some better ones or if they want to check that their weakest chosen student is better than another college's rejected student – a sort of moderation process.

Porter's lodge – Your first port of call at an Oxford or Cambridge college This is where post gets delivered and where, if you get lost, they will be able to direct you – a bit like a reception.

Read – Similarly, instead of 'studying' a subject, the verb used is to 'read' a subject.

Sub fusc – The black gown, black trousers/skirt and white shirts Oxford students must wear to take exams

Summon – Another way to say 'to be called' for interview

Supervision – A class held on a one-to-one basis or in a small group with your tutor (in Cambridge)

Tripos – Word used to describe how Cambridge degree courses are divided into blocks of one or two years called Part I and Part II

Tute – The Oxford slang for a tutorial

Tutorial – A class held on a one-to-one basis or in a small group with your tutor. 'Tutorial' is the word used for this in Oxford

Appendix 2   Key dates

Check these pages regularly to see if you are on track.

■ The year before you are going to apply

September

- Write your 'dream Personal Statement' (see Chapter 3).
- Start log book of lectures and events you have attended and books you have read.
- Start current-affairs diary.

October

- Design your revision timetable.

November

- Revise very hard for your A levels.

January

- Sit A-level modules.

March

- Order undergraduate prospectus from both Oxford and Cambridge and also the alternative prospectus from the student unions of both universities.
- Book yourself on an open day.
- Research other universities to which you are considering applying (you need to choose four).

April

- Write first draft of Personal Statement.
- Go on an open day.

Easter

- Revise very hard for your A levels.

June

- Sit A-level modules.

Summer

- Ask friends and family to read Personal Statement and make revisions.
- Undertake work experience or voluntary work.

■ The year in which you apply

September

- Ask your teacher to read Personal Statement.
- Log in to UCAS and get a username and password.
- Fill in the UCAS form (UCAS applications may be submitted from 1 September).
- Register for the LNAT.
- Book a time to sit the LNAT.
- LNAT (for people who want to study Law at Oxford or Cambridge) can be taken on a date to suit you from the beginning of September.
- Register for the BMAT exam if you are applying for Medicine (at Oxford or Cambridge) or Veterinary Science (Cambridge only).

October

- Fill in separate Oxford Application Form and the Cambridge Supplementary Application Questionnaire (the latter will be emailed to you).
- The deadline for UCAS and Oxford *receiving* your application forms is 15 October. UCAS form and Cambridge Supplementary Application Questionnaire are submitted online. Post Oxford form at least two days before this date (post it 'special delivery' – ask your post office or school).

Late October

- Revise very hard for your A levels.
- Receive acknowledgement letter from your chosen college.
- Sit the appropriate Aptitude test for your subject if there is one:
  - □ BMAT exam (the actual date varies from year to year but is at the end of October or beginning of November) if you are applying for Medicine (at Oxford or Cambridge) or Veterinary Science (Cambridge only).
  - □ HAT (for History applicants to Oxford)
  - □ Physics and Maths for Physics Aptitude test (for Physics or Physics and Philosophy applicants to Oxford)
  - □ ELAT (for applicants to English at Oxford)
  - □ PPEAT (for applicants to PPE at Oxford)
  - □ Maths Aptitude Test (for applicants for Mathematics or Computer Science to Oxford)

November

- Early November – Sit the exams above if they fall in early November and not late October.
- Deadline for sitting LNAT (for people who want to study Law at Oxford or Cambridge) is at the beginning of November.
- Receive letter inviting you to interview from Oxford or Cambridge and explaining if and when to submit written work.

- Submit written work with special form – see faculty website for details. (Work should be sent directly to the college unless you have made an 'open application' in which case send directly to the faculty.) (The work should be marked by your school).

December

- If invited, attend interview (most interviews are held in the first three weeks of December) (see precise interview dates for your subject in the prospectus).
- You may have to sit some tests at interview.
- At Cambridge you may have to sit the TSA.
- Before 25 December – hear outcome of application from Oxford.

January

- Beginning of January – applicants who have been placed in the 'winter pool' are notified (Cambridge only). This may or may not entail going to Cambridge for another set of interviews.
- Middle of January – hear outcome of application from Cambridge
- Sit A-level modules.

Easter

- Revise very hard for your A levels.

June

- Sit A level modules
- After A levels sit STEP paper (Maths only) or AEAs.

August

- Mid-August: results day
- If you have made your grades your place will be confirmed by the university.
- If you have not made your grades, contact the admissions tutor for your college.
- If your college rejects you follow the advice in Chapter 9.

Appendix 3   Open day/college visit table

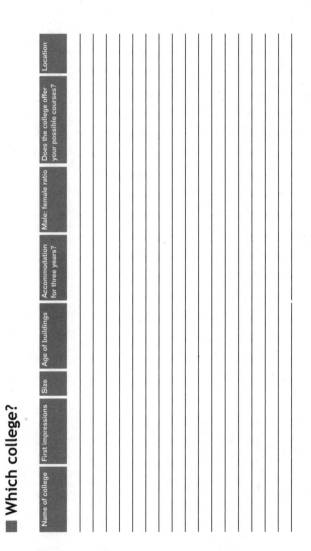

Which college?

Name of college	First impressions	Size	Age of buildings	Accommodation for three years?	Male: female ratio	Does the college offer your possible courses?	Location

Appendix 4 List of colleges and some special features

Overleaf is a table, listing the various colleges in Oxford and Cambridge and their important, and in some cases, unique features.

(The Table follows on the next several pages)

■ Oxford colleges

	Age of college: Old (built before 1800s), Medium (built in 1800s or first part of 1900s), New (built from 1950s onwards)	Size of college: Large (about 400 undergraduates), Medium (about 300), Small (less than 200)	Location	Special features I	Special features II
Balliol College	Old	Large	Central	Has a nursery	
Brasenose College	Old	Large	Central	Next to library	
Christ Church	Old	Large	Central	Has its own meadow and cathedral	Accommodation for all 3–4 years
Corpus Christi College	Old	Small	Central		
Exeter College	Old	Medium	Central	Near library	
Harris Manchester College	Old	Small	Central	Near Science area	Only mature students over 21
Hertford College	Old	Large	Central	Near library	
Jesus College	Old	Medium	Central	Near library	
Keble College	Medium	Large	Opposite University Parks	Near Science area	

College	Age	Size	Location	Feature	Special feature
Lady Margaret Hall	Medium	Large	Far from city centre	Lovely grounds	Was the first women's college in
Lincoln College	Old	Medium	Central	Near library	
Magdalen College	Old	Large	Central	End of High Street	Has its own deer park, lovely grounds
Mansfield College	Medium	Small	Quite central	Near Science area	
Merton College	Old	Medium	Central	Nice food	Lovely grounds
New College	Old	Large	Central	Near Science area and library	
Oriel College	Old	Medium	Central		
Pembroke College	Old	Large	Central	Opposite Christ Church	
The Queen's College	Old	Medium	Central		
St Anne's College	Medium	Large	Far from centre	Has a nursery	Near University Parks
St Catherine's College	New	Large	Far from city centre		
St Edmund Hall	Old	Large	Central	Has a graveyard in the college – interesting grounds	

(Continued)

(Continued)

	Age of college: Old (built before 1800s), Medium (built in 1800s or first part of 1900s), New (built from 1950s onwards)	Size of college: Large (about 400 undergraduates), Medium (about 300), Small (less than 200)	Location	Special features I	Special features II
St Hilda's College	Medium	Large	Far from city centre	Used to be all female but started to admit boys from Oct 2008	Lovely grounds
St Hugh's College	Medium	Large	Far from city centre		
St John's College	Old	Large	Central	Near library	
St Peter's College	New	Large	Central	Near the Oxford Union	
Somerville College	Medium	Large	Far from city centre	Has a nursery	
Trinity College	Old	Medium	Central	Lovely grounds	Near library
University College	Old	Large	Central	Oldest college in Oxford	
Wadham College	Old	Large	Central	Near Science area and library	
Worcester College	Old	Large	Near Oriental Institute, Said business school and train station	Lovely grounds and lake	

Oxford Permanent Private Halls (The bold indicates that they take undergraduates who are not mature students)					
Blackfriars	Only offers Theology and Philosophy	Very small	Central	Dominican order	Mature students
Campion Hall	Mainly a graduate college	Very small	Near Christ Church	Jesuit order	Male only
Regent's Park College	Wide range of subjects and train ministers	Large (for a PPH)	Near library	Baptist foundation	Like a 'normal' small college undergraduate
St Benet's Hall	Classics, English, History and Theology	Large (for a PPH)	Near Little Clarendon Street	Benedictine order	Male only undergraduate
St Stephen's House	Only offers Theology and Philosophy, for people who want to be ordained. For mature students over 25	Medium (for a PPH)	Far from city centre	Anglican foundation	Mature
Wycliffe Hall	Only offers Theology and Philosophy, for people who want to be ordained	Large (for a PPH)	Far from city centre	Anglican foundation	Students with families welcome mature

Cambridge colleges

	Age of college: Old (built before 1800s), Medium (built in 1800s or first part of 1900s), New (built from 1950s onwards)	Size of college: Large (about 400 undergraduates), Medium (about 300), Small (less than 200)	Location Key: Quite Central: ten minute walk to centre	Special features I	Special features II
Christ's College	Old	Large	In city centre	Gives EE offer	
Churchill College	New	Largest college	Not in city centre		Operates a shared nursery
Clare College	Old	Large	City centre	Riverside	
Corpus Christi College	Old	Very small	Central		
Downing College	Medium	Large	Not central		Science area
Emmanuel College	Old	Large	City centre		
Fitzwilliam College	New	Large	Not in centre		Near Science area
Girton College	Medium	Large	Not in centre, 2 miles out of centre	Used to be women only	Operates a shared nursery
Gonville & Caius College	Old	Large	Central	Pronounced 'Keys'; top of academic table	Has a nursery
Homerton College	New	Large	Not in centre		

Hughes Hall	Medium	Very small	Not in centre	Mostly graduate, 89 mature undergraduates
Jesus College	Old	Large	Quite central	Very sporty
King's College	Old	Large	Central	Left wing	Great for music due to their chapel
Lucy Cavendish College	New	Small	Not in centre	Was women only – mature students only
Magdalene College	Old	Large	Central	Traditional	Riverside – own punts
New Hall	New	Large	Not in city centre	All female
Newnham College	Medium	Large	Quite central	All female	Very close to library
Pembroke College	Old	Large	City centre
Peterhouse	Oldest	Medium	Quite central	Accommodation for all 3–4 years	Near Science area
Queens' College	Old	Large	City centre	On the riverside	Has a nursery
Robinson College	New	Large	Quite central	Close to library
St Catharine's College	Old	Large	City centre

(Continued)

(Continued)

College	Age of college: Old (built before 1800s), Medium (built in 1800s or first part of 1900s), New (built from 1950s onwards)	Size of college: Large (about 400 undergraduates), Medium (about 300), Small (less than 200)	Location Key: Quite Central: ten minute walk to centre	Special features I	Special features II
St Edmund's College	Medium	Small	Quite central	Primarily a graduate college but takes mature undergraduates over 21	Small
St John's College	Old	Large	Central	Accommodation for all 3–4 years / Great sporting facilities	Riverside
Selwyn College	Medium	Large	Quite central		Near Languages / Near library
Sidney Sussex College	Old	Large	City centre	Strong facilities for music	

Trinity College	Old	Large	Largest college in centre	Very rich – good facilities and bursaries	Riverside
Trinity Hall	Old	Large	Central	Accommodation for all 3 years	Top of the Tompkin league table
Wolfson College	New	Small	Central	Graduate college admits mature over 21 undergraduates	

Appendix 5　Interview questions

The following questions have been based on pp.103–114, *Getting into Oxford and Cambridge* 10th edition, but have been expanded and updated. The key is that you have to be totally familiar with your A-level subjects and be willing to apply methods and facts you have learnt in your A-level course in unfamiliar settings and situations.

■ General interview questions

- Why this college?
- What are you intending to do in your gap year?
- Summarise your Personal Statement.
- Excluding your A-level reading, what were the last three books you read?
- I notice that you have a grade B in Biology GCSE. Should we be worried about that?
- Give a critical appraisal of the main broadsheet newspaper that you read.
- What do you regard as your strengths and weaknesses?
- What extracurricular activities would you pursue at this college?
- Do you realise that you have applied for the most popular college at this university?
- Why did you make an 'open application'?
- Give us three reasons why we should offer you a place.
- What will you do if we don't?
- What are the synergies, if any, between your three A-level subjects/ why did you choose your A-level subjects?
- So, is it the case that you only want to come to this university but don't care what you do?
- Why did you choose your A-level subjects?
- Name one weakness you have and explain how you would rectify it.
- How will this degree help in your chosen career?
- Do you believe that you have an adventurous side?
- Do you find it daunting not knowing what you will be doing in four or five years' time?
- How would your friends describe you?
- Why are you having to retake your A level(s)? What happened last year?

■ Specialist interview questions

Anthropology/Archaeology

- How do you feel about having to study both Anthropology and Archaeology during your first year before choosing one?
- Name the six major world religions.
- Does Stonehenge mean anything to you?
- What are the problems regarding objectivity in anthropological studies?
- Why do civilisations erect monuments?
- Why should we approach all subjects from a holistic, anthropological perspective?

Art History

- What do we look for when we study Art? What are we trying to reveal?
- Comment on this painting on the wall.
- Compare and contrast these three images.
- What exhibitions have you been to recently?
- How can you classify whether a piece of art is successful or not?
- Do we theorise too much about art?
- Why History of Art?
- How does History of Art help you to break down barriers and communicate with people?
- Does knowing languages help you communicate with the inhabitants of the country?
- Compare the study of the Renaissance with that of the French Revolution.
- Apart from your studies, how else might you pursue your interest in Art History while at the university?

Biochemistry

- Questions on catalysts, enzymes and the chemistry of the formation of proteins
- Questions on oxidation, equilibria and interatomic forces
- Questions on X-ray crystallography
- Why do you wish to read Biochemistry rather than Chemistry?
- Current issues in Biochemistry

Biological Sciences

- How does the immune system recognise invading pathogens as foreign cells?
- How does a cell stop itself from exploding due to osmosis?
- Why is carbon of such importance in living systems?
- How would you transfer a gene to a plant?
- Explain the mechanism of capillary action.

- What are the advantages of the human genome project?
- How would you locate a gene in a nucleus of a cell for a given characteristic?
- What is the major problem with heart transplants in the receiver?
- How does the transplant receiver respond to foreign heart cells?
- How does the body recognise and distinguish its own cells from the foreign cells after a transplant?

Chemistry

- Questions on organic mechanisms
- Questions on structure, bonding and energetics
- Questions on acids and bases
- Questions on isomerisation
- Questions on practical chemical analysis
- See also Biochemistry questions.

Classics

- Questions on classical civilisation and literature
- Why do you think Ancient History is important?
- How civilised was the Roman world?
- Apart from your A-level texts, what have you read in the original or in translation?

Earth Sciences and Geology

- Where would you place this rock sample in geological time?
- How would you determine a rock's age?
- Can you integrate this decay curve, and why would the result be useful?
- Questions on Chemistry
- When do you think oil will run out?

Economics

- Explain how the Phillips curve arises.
- Would it be feasible to have an economy which was entirely based on the service sector?
- A man pays for his holiday at a hotel on a tropical island by cheque. He has a top credit rating and rather than cashing it, the hotelier pays a supplier using the same cheque. That supplier does the same thing with one of his suppliers and so on ad infinitum. Who pays for the man's holiday?
- Discuss the interaction between fiscal and monetary policy.
- I notice that you study Mathematics. Can you see how you might derive the profit maximisation formula from first principles?
- Discuss competition in the TV industry.
- How effective is current monetary policy?

- What are your particular interests as regards economics?
- Do you think we should worry about a balance of payments deficit?
- If you were the Chancellor of the Exchequer, how would you maximise tax revenue?
- If you had a fairy godmother who gave you unlimited sums of money, what sort of company would you start and what types of employee would you hire?
- What are the advantages and disadvantages of joining the Euro?
- What are the qualities of a good economist?
- Why are you studying Economics A level?
- What would happen to employment and wage rates if the pound depreciated?
- Do you the think the Chinese exchange rate will increase?
- How does the housing market affect inflation?
- How has social mobility changed in recent times?

Engineering

- Questions on Mathematics and Physics, particularly Calculus and Mechanics
- Questions on mathematical derivations, for example, of laws of motion
- This mechanical system sitting on my desk – how does it work?
- How do aeroplanes fly?
- What is impedance matching and how can it be achieved?
- How do bicycle spokes work?
- How would you divide a tetrahedron into two identical parts?
- What is the total resistance of the tetrahedron if there are resistors of one ohm on each edge?
- Questions on Hooke's law.

English

- What defines a novel as Gothic?
- What is the most important work of literature of the twentieth century?
- Who is your favourite author?
- Do you do any creative writing? Do you keep a diary? Do you write letters?
- Discussion of reading beyond your A-level texts
- Provide a review of the last Shakespeare play you saw at the theatre.
- Examine the hypothesis that Shakespeare was unusually atheistic for his time.
- Questions on deconstruction of a poem
- Questions on the use of language
- Are Iago and Othello good listeners?
- Discuss the last novel you read.

Geography

- Is Geography just a combination of other disciplines?
- Why should it be studied in its own right?
- Would anything remain of Geography if we took the notion of place off the syllabus?
- How important is the history of towns when studying settlement patterns?
- Why is climate so unpredictable?
- What is the importance of space in global warming?
- Why do you think people care about human geography more than physical geography? What is more important mapping or computer models?
- If you went to an isolated island to do research on the beach how would you use the local community?
- Analyse a graph about a river. Why are there peaks and troughs?
- Look at a world map showing quality of life indicators. Explain the pattern in terms of two of the indicators.
- See also questions on Land Economy.

History

- Questions on historical themes and movements
- How can one define revolution?
- Why did imperialism happen?
- What were the differences between German and Italian unification?
- Who was the greater democrat – Gladstone or Disraeli?
- Was the fall of the Weimar Republic inevitable?
- 'History is the study of the present with the benefit of hindsight.' Discuss.
- Would history be worth studying if it didn't repeat itself?
- What is the difference between Modern History and Modern Politics?
- What is the position of the individual in history?
- Would you abolish the monarchy for ideological or practical reasons?
- Should we abolish the House of Lords?
- Should we elect the second chamber?
- Why do historians differ in their views on Hitler?
- What skills should a historian have?
- In what periods has the Holy Grail been popular, with whom and why?
- Why do you think the Holy Grail gains more attention during certain periods?
- Why is it important to visit historical sites relevant to the period you are studying?

Human Sciences

- Discuss BSE and its implications, and the role of prions in CJD.
- What causes altitude sickness and how do humans adapt physiologically to high altitudes?

- Discuss exploitation of indigenous populations by Westerners.
- Why is statistics a useful subject for human scientists?
- Why are humans so difficult to experiment with?
- Design an experiment to determine whether genetics or upbringing is more important.
- What are the scientific implications of globalisation on the world?

Land Economy

- Will the UK lose its sovereignty if it joins EMU?
- Will EMU encourage regionalism?
- Will the information technology revolution gradually result in the death of inner cities?
- What has been the effect of the Channel tunnel on surrounding land use?

Law

- Questions on written cases, judgements and arguments.
- Questions on the points of law arising from scenarios – often relating to criminal law or duty of care.
- A cyclist rides the wrong way down a one-way street and a chimney falls on him. What legal proceedings should he take?
- What if he is riding down a private drive signed 'no trespassing'?
- X intends to poison his wife but accidentally gives the lethal draught to her identical twin. Murder?
- Questions on legal issues, particularly current ones
- Should stalking be a criminal offence?
- Should judges have a legislative role?
- Do you think that anyone should be able to serve on a jury?
- Should judges be elected?
- Do judges have political bias?
- To what extent do you think the press should be able to release information concerning allegations against someone?
- Is there anything you want to discuss or that you're really interested in?
- Euthanasia – who has the right to decide?
- How does the definition of intent distinguish murder from manslaughter?
- Can you give a definition of murder and manslaughter?
- Should foresight of consequences be considered as intending such consequences?

Material Sciences

- Questions on Physics, particularly solid materials
- Questions on Mathematics, particularly forces
- Investigations of sample materials, particularly structure and fractures.

Mathematics and Computation

- Questions (which may become progressively harder) on almost any area of A-level Maths and Further Maths
- Pure maths questions on integration
- Applied maths questions on forces
- Statistics questions on probability
- Computation questions on iterations, series and computer arithmetic.

Medicine

- What did your work experience teach you about life as a doctor?
- What did you learn about asthma in your work experience on asthma research?
- How have doctors' lives changed in the last 30 years?
- Explain the logic behind the most recent of the NHS reforms.
- Discuss the mechanisms underlying diabetes.
- Why is it that cancer cells are more susceptible to destruction by radiation than normal cells?
- How would you determine whether leukaemia patients have contracted the disease because of a nearby nuclear power station?
- What does isometric exercise mean in the context of muscle function?
- Discuss the mechanisms underlying sensory adaptation.
- What is an ECG?
- Why might a GP not prescribe antibiotics to a toddler?
- Why are people anxious before surgery? Is it justifiable?
- How do you deal with stress?
- Questions on gene therapy
- Questions on the ethics of foetal transplantation
- Questions on Biochemistry and Human Biology.

Modern Languages

- Tests and questions on comprehension and translation
- Reading tests
- Questions which focus on the use of language in original texts
- Describe aspects of a poem (that was given to the candidate before the interview) which you find interesting.
- Interpret a poem, commenting about tone and the context of the poem.
- Why do you want to study your language and not another?
- Why is it important to study literature?
- What is the difference between literature and philosophy?
- What French book have I recently read that I enjoyed?
- French conversation talking about a work placement in Le Touquet
- Questions on cultural and historical context and genre in European literature
- How important is analysis of narrative in the study of literature?
- How important is biography in the study of literature?

Natural Sciences

- What is an elastic collision?
- What happens when two particles collide – one moving and one stationary?
- What is friction?
- Questions on carboxylic acids.

Oriental Studies

- What do you know about the Chinese language and its structure?
- What are the differences between English and any Oriental language with which you are familiar?
- Compare and contrast any ambiguities in the following sentences:
  - Only suitable magazines are sold here.
  - Many species inhabit a small space.
  - He is looking for the man who crashed his car.
- Comment on the following sentences:
  - He did wrong.
  - He was wrong.
  - He was about to do wrong.

Philosophy

- What is Philosophy?
- Give examples of philosophical questions.
- Would you agree that if p is true and s believes p, then s knows p?
- Is the above a question about knowing or a question about the meaning of the word know?
- Discuss:
  - I could be dreaming that I am in this interview.
  - I do not know whether I am dreaming or not.
  - Therefore I do not know whether I am in this interview or not.
- Can a m.achine have free will?
- When I see red, could I be seeing what you see when you see green?
- Is it a matter of fact or logic that time travels in one direction only?
- Is our faith in scientific method itself based on scientific method? If so, does it matter?
- I can change my hairstyle and still be me. I can change my political opinions and still be me. I can have a sex change and still be me. What is it then that makes me be me?
- Can it ever be morally excusable to kill someone?

Physics

- Questions on Applied Mathematics
- Questions on any aspect of the Physics syllabus
- Questions on mathematical derivations
- How does glass transmit light?

- How does depressing a piano key make a sound?
- How does the voltage on a capacitor vary if the dielectric gas is ionised?

Politics

- Define government. Why do we need governments?
- Differentiate between power and authority.
- Distinguish between a society, a state and an economy.
- Will Old Labour ever be revived? If so, under what circumstances?
- Why do you think that Communism was unsuccessful in the Russian countryside?
- What would you say to someone who claims that women already have equal opportunities?
- What would you do tomorrow if you were the president of the former Soviet Union?
- How does a democracy work?
- What constitute the ideologies of the extreme right?
- Does the extreme right pose a threat to other less extreme parties?
- What do you think of Labour's discrimination in favour of female parliamentarians?
- How would you improve the comprehensive system of education?

Politics, Philosophy and Economics

- Define power, authority and influence.
- How important is national identity? What is the Scottish national identity?
- Should medics pay more for their degrees?
- What is the difference in the mentality of Americans in 1760 and 1770?

Psychology

- Questions on Neurophysiology
- Questions on Statistics
- Questions on the experimental elucidation of the mechanisms underlying behaviour
- Give some examples of why an understanding of Chemistry might be important in Psychology.
- A new treatment is tested on a group of depressives, who are markedly better in six weeks. Does this show that the treatment was effective?
- There are records of violent crimes that exactly mimic scenes of violence on TV. Does this indicate that TV causes real violence?
- How would you establish the quietest sound that you can hear as opposed to the quietest sound that you think you can hear?
- Why might one be able to remember items at the beginning and end

of an aurally presented list better than items in the middle?
- Could a computer ever feel emotion?
- Is it ethically justifiable to kill animals for the purpose of research?
- What is emotional intelligence?

Social and Political Sciences

- What is the value of the study of Social Anthropology?
- Do people need tabloids?
- How would you define terrorism?
- Do you believe in selective education? Are we participating in selective education here?
- Is it possible to pose a sociological problem without sociological bias?
- Does prison work?
- Are MPs only in it for the power?
- What aspects of the subject are you particularly looking forward to studying?
- See also questions on Politics.

Theology

- Does moral rectitude reside in the agent, the act or its consequences?
- What, if anything, is wrong with voluntary euthanasia?
- What is the best reason that you can think of for believing in the existence of God?
- Do you think that this course could conceivably be persuasive on the issue?
- What relevance does Theology have for Art History?
- What relevance does Archaeology have for Theology?
- Comment on the portrayal of Jesus in *John* versus the other gospels.

Veterinary Medicine

- Should the veterinary profession show positive discrimination in favour of men?
- Has your work experience influenced your future career aspirations?
- Discuss any aspect of animal physiology which has struck you as contrasting with what you know of human physiology.
- Would our knowledge of BSE have been of value in controlling foot-and-mouth disease?
- Discuss the biochemistry of DNA.
- What animal did this skull belong to?
- See also questions on Biological Sciences and Chemistry.

Maps

■ Oxford map

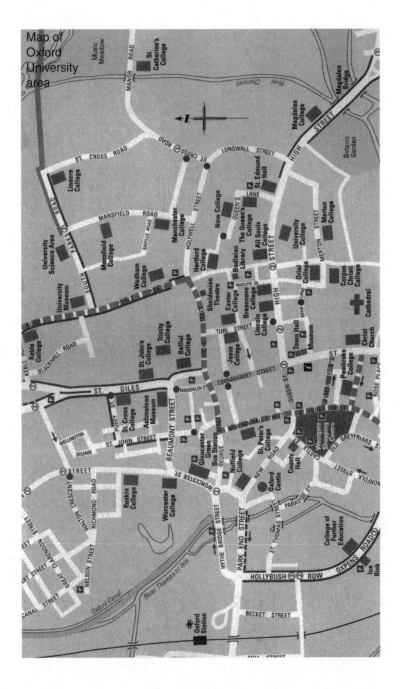

Map of Oxford University area

Cambridge map

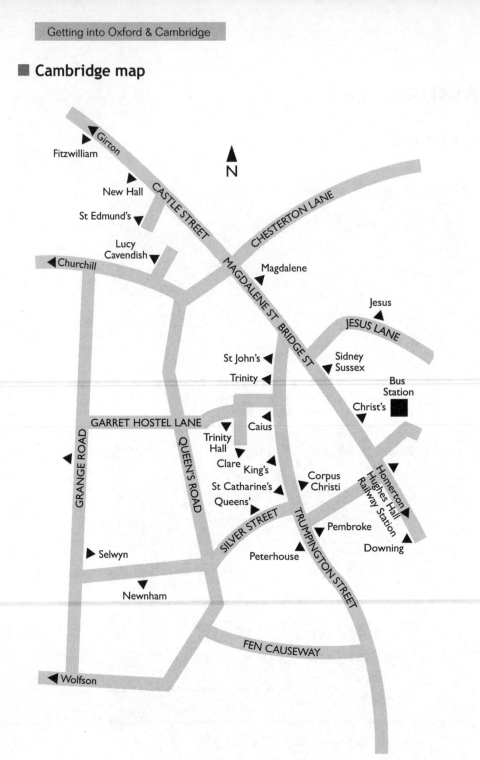

Postscript

If you have followed the advice in this book then you will have certainly given Oxford or Cambridge your best shot. Good luck and remember that you will be successful at whichever university you attend.

Natalie Lancer

MPW (London)
90-92 Queen's Gate
London
SW7 5AB
Tel: 020 7835 1355
Fax: 020 7225 2953
Email: enquiries@mpw.co.uk